Introduction

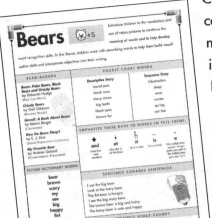

Children are born with the innate desire to communicate. In the early years, they label, mimic, and experiment with language. As they develop and grow, there is a natural tendency for them to expand their love of language into written expression; first through random scribbles and symbols, and then with specific words and sentences. Yet, when many of these children come to school, they are expected to use formal writing before they are ready. When children do not yet possess the prerequisites for writing, they may become frustrated and discouraged and may have the desire to give up trying to write.

Successful writing requires four key elements:

- the desire to say something
- the vocabulary to say it
- the ability to make words
- the structure with which to say it

As young children are acquiring these prerequisites, they need support and direction. It is important to be able to determine each child's developmental level and provide activities that will serve as building blocks to help children internalize the writing process.

Rebuses are a great way to provide children with the tools they need in order to learn to write. Rebuses are a wonderful way of combining pictures and print. Children quickly learn that words are meant to convey meaning. The use of rebuses exposes children to words that are above their reading level but part of their spoken vocabulary. As young children work with rebuses, they begin to understand the reading process and how decoding and encoding work. They also develop strong print awareness and utilize their own written language to practice their emerging reading skills. With the support of rebus vocabulary, beginning writers are empowered with the tools they need to express themselves in print.

The rebuses used throughout the program presented in *Rebus Writing* are designed to teach word meaning, expand vocabulary, and provide orthographic support. The rebuses incorporate pictures and phonetic units. By having to combine the elements in the picture, children are actually sounding out the rebus and developing their decoding and encoding skills.

Rebus Writing features seasonal themes that integrate content learning and writing. The integrated themes include science, social studies, and seasonal concepts. Each theme introduces related vocabulary, the printed word, and a pictorial rebus to teach children about the concept and provide the words they need to write sentences and related stories. Additionally, since many of the rebus activities are based on beginning reading skills, these activities can be incorporated into reading instruction.

The rebus vocabulary and themes start out very simple. This allows children to immediately recognize a specific word and its meaning. As children become competent with the rebus format, the vocabulary and rebuses become more involved. Children experiencing rebus for the first time may respond differently than their peers. The youngest children, when asked to write, may only copy the vocabulary words from the dictionary. Other children may add the rebus pictures for the words they write. The rebus pictures are very simple so that children can readily reproduce them. Children draw the rebus to reinforce the meaning of each word and to guarantee that they can accurately read what they wrote. As children gain confidence, they begin to combine words and write sentences.

At the beginning, emphasis is placed on adjectives so that children can develop their descriptive writing skills—a sentence with describing words or a descriptive story. As the themes progress, nouns, adjectives, and verbs are all used so that children can learn about word functions and expand beyond pattern sentences. The rebus vocabulary, in conjunction with related shared reading and "read aloud" books, gives children the background they need to formulate ideas and facilitate informational writing.

Beginning with the first theme, children cut and paste the rebus vocabulary into a picture dictionary. This provides each child with a "reference book" to use as he or she completes related activities and writes about the theme. Additionally, this vocabulary can be used for phonemic awareness and phonetic development. Use the reproducibles to help children practice the writing process. The multileveled activities will help you meet the needs of children at various writing stages. As a result, all children learn the same content but write about it at their own developmental level.

Providing the building blocks of writing has never been easier!

Spring Rebus Writing

Combining Pictures and Print to Support Beginning Writers

Written by

Jo Fitzpatrick

Editors: Sheri Rous and Carla Hamaguchi
Illustrators: Darcy Tom and Corina Chien
Designer: Moonhee Pak
Cover Designer: Barbara Peterson
Art Director: Tom Cochrane
Project Director: Carolea Williams

Table of Contents

DIRECTED ACTIVITIES

	Intro	Frogs	Leprechauns	Rabbits	Chicks	Plants	Butterflies
Picture Dictionary	13	27	44	62	79	96	113
Word Hunt	14	29	46	64	81	98	115
Secret Sentence Booklet	15	30	47	65	82	99	116
Bubble Writing	16	32	49	67	84	101	118
Connect a Sentence	17	33	50	68	85	102	119
Sentence Squares	18	34	51	69	86	103	120
Sentence/Story Builder	19	35	52	70	87	104	121
Story Box	20	36	53	71	88	105	122
Backward Story	21	37	54	72	89	106	123

INDEPENDENT/CENTER ACTIVITIES

	Intro	Frogs	Leprechauns	Rabbits	Chicks	Plants	Butterflies
Descriptive Story	22	38	55	73	90	107	124
Shape Book	23	39	57	74	91	108	125
Class Book	24	41	59	76	93	110	127
Sequence Story	25	42	60	77	94	111	128

Using Rebus Writing to Differentiate

Learning to write is a developmental process that involves movement through designated writing stages. In order to develop stronger writing skills and move through these levels, children need to understand the writing process and how to express and organize ideas before putting them into print. For many, this is not an automatic or a natural process. Children need guidance and practice before they can easily turn oral language into written language.

To meet the needs of your children, complete the activities as a whole group, in small groups, or independently. They can be done orally with younger writers or collaboratively by writing on an enlarged reproducible page. Or, invite children to work with a partner to create sentences or stories. The independent or center activities include an art project and additional vocabulary. You can easily differentiate the activities to help children work at their own ability level. Use the follow-up activities for more advanced writers.

The activities in *Rebus Writing* are designed to give support to children at each and every beginning writing stage. The developmental activities for each theme use the rebus vocabulary to help children develop and expand their ideas. The activities involve individual student writing using support vocabulary; a Rebus Dictionary, pocket chart words, and related word webs are included in each theme. The level of difficulty can be adjusted to the needs and competency of the children and can range from sentence writing to story development. Beginning writers will become familiar with words and their meaning, while more advanced writers will be able to practice their spelling. Children will gain experience with different writing types: descriptive, narrative, and informational. Emphasis is placed on the following skills:

- sentence formation
- elaboration and expansion of ideas
- cloze completion
- sequence of events
- application of content

Children, no matter their ability level, will have access to the same content and information. They will be able to rely on their skill, interest, and readiness levels to apply this information. Adjust or tier the difficulty and focus of the activities (i.e., producing words, sentences, or stories) to differentiate the instruction based upon developmental needs.

The Rebus Approach provides built-in differentiation. Due to the nature of the program, children are able to use content to become self-improving writers. Young writers take and use the rebus and support activities at "face value" and learn how to use and combine words to develop meaningful sentences. Early writers use the support system to learn how to expand and elaborate ideas and develop related stories. More advanced writers use the Rebus Approach as a springboard to expand the informational content in their writing and to experiment with different writing genres. No matter the writing stage, the Rebus Approach empowers all children to become highly motivated and productive writers.

It is easy to address each child's developmental level. With exposure and practice, children will progress, at their own pace, from simple word writing to sentence and story writing. The activities included in each theme can be adapted accordingly. They can be done orally, as an interactive lesson, or independently for more advanced writers. The scope of the activities ranges from simple to more complex and can be used accordingly with children at various writing stages.

Getting Started

Initially, the rebuses might seem a little overwhelming to you, especially when looking at them in their entirety. However, it is important to remember that children learn the rebuses as they go. As they learn them, so do you. After a while, the graphics become second nature and you will begin to think in terms of rebuses! Use the following steps to make each child's rebus writing experience more memorable.

STEP 1

There are certain standard graphics that form the rebus vocabulary. It is important to be aware of these graphics and what they represent. Review the **Graphics for Phonetic Elements** (page 10), the **Positional Vocabulary** (page 11), and the **Everyday Rebuses** (page 12) to help you internalize the basic graphics that appear in the rebus vocabulary. You can also refer to these lists if you make rebuses for songs, charts, and other materials.

STEP 2

Prepare a **Picture Dictionary** for each child by either purchasing a 40-page, 8½" x 6⅞" (21.5 cm x 18 cm) composition book for each child or placing 40 pieces of blank paper into a folded piece of construction paper and stapling the left side. Write each child's name on the cover of the book. Make a few extra dictionaries in case a new child comes to class during the year. As children work in their dictionary, add the picture cards to the additional dictionaries.

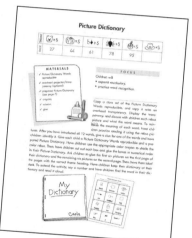

STEP 3

Read aloud a **content-related book** that relates to the theme of study. This will provide children with some background knowledge and give them a chance to hear some of the theme words in context. A list of suggested literature selections is included on the section opener page for each theme of study. Continue reading additional theme-related books throughout the theme to help reinforce it.

STEP 4

Review the **section opener** page for the theme of study. This page provides information about the theme, a list of theme-related literature selections, a list of "Have-To Words," Sequence Story Pocket Chart Words, a Sequence Story Prompt, and Descriptive Story Pocket Chart Words.

STEP 5 As children write about the theme, they use many high-frequency words that are not in their Picture Dictionary. It is important that children spell these words correctly. If left to invented spelling and sounding out, errors will appear, be repeated, and then learned. **Have-To Words** are words that children have to learn to read and spell. These words have been incorporated into each theme and appear throughout the activities. Create a **Have-To Board** on a bulletin board. Write the Have-To Words from the unit of study on separate sentence strips, and attach the sentence strips to the bulletin board. Number the words, and place them in rows of up to five words. Add additional words from other classroom studies, as needed. Have children read and spell the words on the board. If a child needs assistance finding a word, tell the child to look in a specific row or give the child the number of the desired word. As children master each word, remove it from the board.

STEP 6 The **Directed Activities** section (pages 13–21) includes numerous activities and reproducibles that teach and reinforce the rebus words for each theme. Children practice their writing in a whole-class or small-group setting while gaining confidence in their skills.

STEP 7 The **Independent or Writing Center Activities** section (pages 22–25) provides even the youngest writer with an opportunity to use support vocabulary to process information, formulate ideas, and then put those ideas down on paper. The degree of difficulty can be adjusted from simple sentence writing to story development. In each theme, emphasis is placed on descriptive writing, informational writing, and sequential writing. A reproducible is included for each activity. Either have children work independently or in a writing center to complete the activities.

STEP 8 Activities rotate through the themes. For example, each theme has a Word Hunt activity. Read the activity directions (page 14) and use the **Rebus Page Number Box** at the top of each activity to find the accompanying reproducible for the theme you have chosen. For example, the Word Hunt reproducible for the Frogs theme is on page 29.

THEME	🐸 +s	🧑‍🎩 +s	🐰 +s	🐤 +s	🌱 +s	🦋 +s
PAGE	29	46	64	81	98	115

Organizational Tips

Rebus Writing is an extensive resource for teachers of beginning writers. Differentiation and developmental instruction is built right into the program. Everything you need is here, including support materials, instructional word cards, and numerous activities.

All types of student grouping and instructional strategies can be used with the activities in this resource, depending on the range of ability levels in your classroom and your teaching style and preference. You can elect to complete the activities in whole-group, small-group, or independent settings. The following suggestions are made to serve as a springboard to help you design the best organizational plan that meets your children's particular needs.

WHOLE-GROUP INSTRUCTION

- Read-alouds
- Shared reading
- Have-To Words
- Introduction of rebus vocabulary
- Picture Dictionary
- Secret Sentence Booklets
- Bubble Writing
- Connect a Sentence

SMALL-GROUP (SKILL-BASED) INSTRUCTION

Group students according to their developmental needs for these activities:
- Sentence Squares
- Sentence/Story Builder
- Story Box
- Backward Story

SMALL-GROUP (HETEROGENEOUS) INSTRUCTION

Group students in small groups that consist of varied ability levels or as a center activity. Allow advanced students to work independently.
- Descriptive Story
- Shape Book
- Class Book
- Sequence Story

Basic Rebuses

GRAPHICS FOR PHONETIC ELEMENTS

The following graphics are used in many phonetic words to help children learn and apply the decoding process. These phonetic sounds are represented with a rebus that is related to the actual sound. Use the phrase to explain the rebus.

/th/   the stick-out-your-tongue sound

/sh/   the quiet sound

/ou/   the hammerhead sound
(what you say when you hit your finger with a hammer)

/oo/   the ghost sound

/ing/   the king of the *ing* sound

/ch/   the choo choo sound

/oo/   the muscle man sound
(what you say when you lift something heavy)

/er/   hold onto the r (*ir* and *ur*)

/u/   the belly button sound—like when you poke yourself in the belly button
(this is used for the short *u* sound and the schwa sound)

"A" Note: If the rebus is in quotes, say the name of the letter (for use with long vowel sounds). Use this when a letter name is a sound (e.g., /ar/ = "R" or candy = 🥫 + "D").

The following words use the above graphics. Once you get used to the phonetic graphics, you will see how easy it is to come up with rebuses for practically any word you want.

they

each

room

thing

make

town

learn

should

The following rebuses help describe locations. Write the rebuses on the board. As you introduce each rebus, say the phrase so children will understand the graphic.

the dot is **in** the box

the dot is **out** of the box

the dot is **on** the box

the dot is **over** the box

the dot is **under** the box

the dot fell **from** the shelf

the dot is **between** the lines

the dot is **after** the line

the dot is **before** the line

the dot is **at** the line

the dot is at the **top** of the paper

the dot is at the **bottom** of the paper

The following rebuses are used for basic vocabulary. Write the rebuses on the board. Say each phrase when you introduce the rebus to children.

it **is** a line

it is **a** belly button

that means **was**

has—breathe out and say /s/

one circle **with** another

the car **went** down the street

give me the box

I **did** it

who—what an owl says

where in the world are you

it **is** a dot

"R"
it's an **R** for the word are

this says **were**

I **have** the dot

will—/w/ + ill in bed

do—/d/ + the ghost sound

I **gave** him the box

didn't—did + /nt/

what's in the box

"Y"
why—the letter "y"

pointing to **the** ___

it's a **saw**

one line **and** another

I **had** the dot but dropped it

I **want** the dot

the **don't** symbol

some—/s/ + belly button + /m/

I **made** it with my hands

when—day or night

away—belly button + one-way sign

Picture Dictionary

THEME	🐸 +s	🧑‍🦰 +s	🐰 +s	🐥 +s	🌱 +s	🦋 +s
PAGE	27	44	62	79	96	113

MATERIALS

- ✓ Picture Dictionary Words reproducible
- ✓ overhead projector/transparency (optional)
- ✓ prepared Picture Dictionary (see page 7)
- ✓ crayons
- ✓ scissors
- ✓ glue

FOCUS

Children will

- expand vocabulary.
- practice word recognition.

Copy a class set of the Picture Dictionary Words reproducible, and copy it onto an overhead transparency. Display the transparency, and discuss with children each rebus picture and what the word means. To reinforce the meaning of each word, have children practice reading it using the rebus pictures.

After you have introduced all 12 words, give a clue for one of the words and have children identify it. Give each child a Picture Dictionary Words reproducible and a prepared Picture Dictionary. Have children use the appropriate color crayon to shade the color rebus. Then, have children cut out each box and glue the boxes in numerical order in their Picture Dictionary. Ask children to glue the first six pictures on the first page of their dictionary and the remaining six pictures on the second page. Then, have them label the pages with the correct theme heading. Have children keep their dictionary at their desk. To extend the activity, say a number and have children find the word in their dictionary and read it aloud.

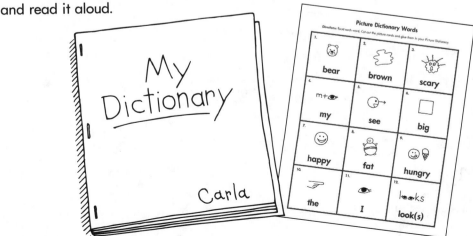

Word Hunt

THEME	🐸 +S	🧑‍🦰 +S	🐰 +S	🐤 +S	🌱 +S	🦋 +S
PAGE	29	46	64	81	98	115

MATERIALS

✓ Word Hunt reproducible

✓ Picture Dictionaries (see page 13)

Children will
- practice word recognition.
- use dictionary skills.

Have children point to each word for the theme of study in their Picture Dictionary as you say the word aloud. Give each child a Word Hunt reproducible. Point to the pictures on the reproducible. Explain to the class that they are to use their Picture Dictionary to locate the matching picture and write the corresponding word on the line underneath the picture on their reproducible. Tell children that at the bottom of the page they will discover a surprise sentence to complete. Point to the bracket and explain that this symbol means to start the sentence with a capital letter. Point to the dot at the end of the sentence. Explain that the dot represents a period and is at the end of a sentence. To extend the activity, write additional sentences on the board for children to complete. Note: Once children understand how to complete the activity, word practice may no longer be necessary.

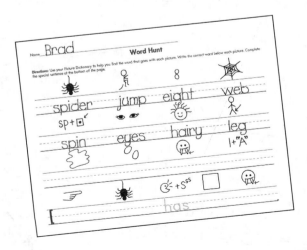

Secret Sentence Booklet

THEME	+ S	+ S	+ S	+ S	+ S	+ S
PAGE	30–31	47–48	65–66	82–83	99–100	116–117

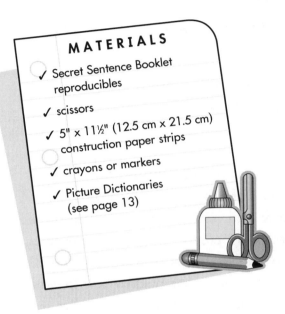

MATERIALS

✓ Secret Sentence Booklet reproducibles

✓ scissors

✓ 5" x 11½" (12.5 cm x 21.5 cm) construction paper strips

✓ crayons or markers

✓ Picture Dictionaries (see page 13)

FOCUS

Children will
- expand vocabulary.
- write sentences.

Copy the Secret Sentence Booklet reproducibles for each child. Cut the reproducibles in half lengthwise on the line. Assemble them in numerical order. Staple the left side of a construction paper strip to the front and back of the reproducibles to make a booklet. Give each child a prepared Secret Sentence Booklet. Draw a rebus sentence (pictures only) from the reproducible on the board. Point to each rebus picture, and have children say the word that goes with the rebus. Next, write the word under the picture. Read the word for the picture. Emphasize to children that the word is written right under the picture to allow for space between words. Continue adding each remaining word under the correct rebus picture. Have children count the rebus pictures and words on the board. Ask them to open their Secret Sentence Booklet. Point to the bracket in the booklet and remind children that this symbol means to start the sentence with a capital letter. Have children trace each bracket with a green crayon or marker. Then, point to the dot at the end of each sentence and remind children that the dot represents a period and is the end of a sentence. Have children color each period with a red crayon or marker. Invite them to read the first rebus sentence in their booklet to discover what the Secret Sentence says. Have children use their Picture Dictionary to help them write each word under the appropriate picture. Have children complete one sentence in their booklet each day until they have completed all the sentences. Encourage them to read aloud their sentences.

Bubble Writing

THEME	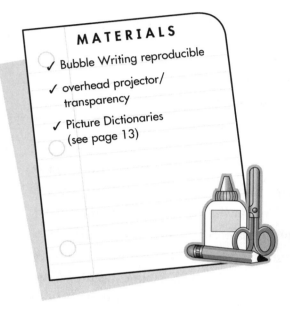 +S	+S	+S	+S	+S	+S
PAGE	32	49	67	84	101	118

MATERIALS

✓ Bubble Writing reproducible

✓ overhead projector/ transparency

✓ Picture Dictionaries (see page 13)

FOCUS

Children will

• practice word recognition.

• write sentences.

Copy a class set of the Bubble Writing reproducible. Copy it onto an overhead transparency, and display the transparency. Give each child a reproducible. Point to the pictures in the bubbles. Invite volunteers to "read" each rebus. Model for children how to write the words for the rebuses. Have children use their Picture Dictionary to help them write the correct word next to each bubble. Explain to children that each blank in the sentence has a number that corresponds with the numbered bubbles. Show children how to use the numbered words in the bubbles to complete the numbered cloze sentences on the bottom of the page. Invite volunteers to read aloud the completed sentences.

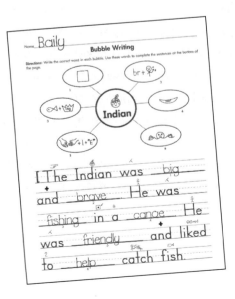

Connect a Sentence

THEME	🐸 +S	🧙 +S	🐰 +S	🐤 +S	🌱 +S	🦋 +S
PAGE	33	50	68	85	102	119

MATERIALS

✓ Connect a Sentence reproducible

✓ overhead projector/ transparency

✓ writing paper

✓ crayons (optional)

FOCUS

Children will

- write pattern sentences.
- expand rebus vocabulary.
- combine ideas.

Copy a class set of the Connect a Sentence reproducible. Copy it onto an overhead transparency, and display the transparency. Discuss the rebus pictures and their word meaning with the class. Give each child a reproducible. Have children combine the phrase in the center bubble with words from the connecting bubbles to create sentences and write them on a piece of paper. Explain to children that they need to choose words that make sense in a sentence. Ask if it makes sense to say *The bear looks funny and cute.* (yes) Ask if it makes sense to say *The bear looks big and little.* (no) Encourage children to combine words from more than one bubble to expand their sentences. To extend the activity, choose a word that appears in a bubble and have children trace the bubble with a given color crayon. Repeat this process with seven additional bubbles and crayons. Say a color or invite a volunteer to say a color, and have children read the center bubble and then add the word that appears in the corresponding color bubble. For example, if you say the color red, children read the center bubble and then finish the sentence with the text that appears in the red bubble (e.g., *The bear looks hungry*).

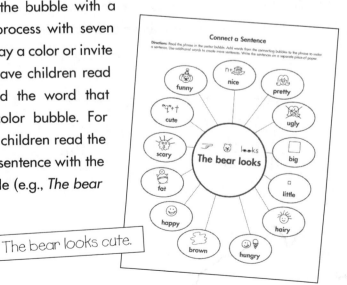

The bear looks cute.

Sentence Squares

THEME	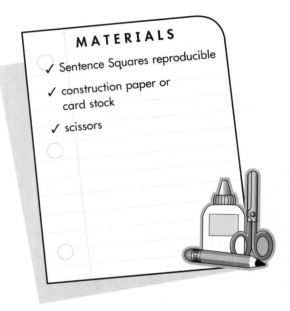 🐸 + s	🎩 + s	🐰 + s	🐤 + s	🌱 + s	🦋 + s
PAGE	34	51	69	86	103	120

MATERIALS

✓ Sentence Squares reproducible

✓ construction paper or card stock

✓ scissors

FOCUS

Children will practice sentence formation.

Copy a class set of the Sentence Squares reproducible onto construction paper or card stock for durability. Give each child a reproducible. Have children cut apart their squares. Say a short sentence that includes words from the reproducible. (Sample sentences are listed on the section opener page for the theme of study.) Have children select the appropriate word squares and arrange them in the correct order to make the sentence. Begin by saying the whole sentence, and then repeat the sentence a few words at a time as children find the squares to make that part of the sentence. Remind children that each sentence begins with a capital letter and ends with a punctuation mark. Repeat the process with additional sentences. To extend the activity, have children use their squares to make up their own sentences. As an option, send home the activity as homework, and have children bring back a list of the sentences they made.

Look at the funny bear

Sentence/Story Builder

THEME	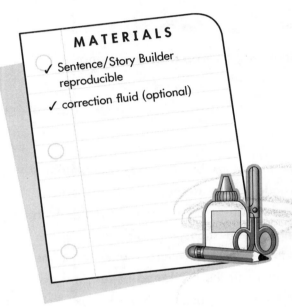 +S	+S	+S	+S	+S	+S
PAGE	35	52	70	87	104	121

MATERIALS

✓ Sentence/Story Builder reproducible

✓ correction fluid (optional)

FOCUS

Children will develop a structured sentence or story.

Give each child a Sentence/Story Builder reproducible. Discuss the illustrations that describe *who, what, when, where,* and *why.* Help children use the illustrations to develop a sentence or story that includes these elements. Ask questions to help guide the sequence of the story and provide transition. For younger writers, concentrate on the composing process so children see how to connect ideas. For more advanced writers, help children formulate their ideas and model the writing process. When children are ready, have them complete the activity independently. To extend the activity, use correction fluid to delete the pictures and text from the "Is Doing What" and "Why" boxes. Have children add their own words and illustrations to these boxes and then write a story. Remind children that all sentences begin with a capital letter and end with a punctuation mark.

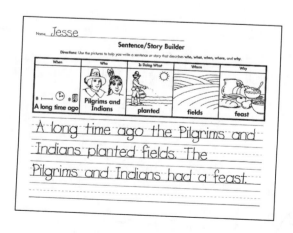

Story Box

THEME	🐸 +s	🧔 +s	🐰 +s	🐤 +s	🌿 +s	🦋 +s
PAGE	36	53	71	88	105	122

MATERIALS

✓ Story Box reproducible

✓ overhead transparency/ projector

✓ crayons (optional)

FOCUS

Children will develop a story sequence.

Copy the Story Box reproducible onto an overhead transparency, and display it. Discuss with the class the character(s) and the setting. Ask questions to help children expand their thinking. Direct children's attention to the illustrations in the numbered boxes, and discuss what is happening in each box. Help children use these three pictures to combine their ideas into a sequential story. Present the activity orally with emerging writers and as a guided writing lesson with more advanced writers. Ask children questions about the illustrations to help guide the sequence of events and provide transition. As children become more comfortable with these procedures, have them complete the activity independently. Provide a list of transition words (e.g., *once, first, then, next, finally, because*) to help them connect their ideas. To extend the activity, have more capable writers illustrate their own Story Box reproducible and write a story based upon the illustrations and picture sequence.

Backward Story

THEME	+S	+S	+S	+S	+S	+S
PAGE	37	54	72	89	106	123

MATERIALS

✓ Backward Story reproducible

FOCUS

Children will understand story components and sequence.

Introduce the activity by reading aloud the end of the story as it appears on the Backward Story reproducible. Ask questions related to the story's ending to help children develop ideas for a beginning and middle. (Sample questions can be found on the reproducible.) Use the information gathered from the class discussion to help children orally organize a theme-related story with a beginning, middle, and ending. Have more advanced writers write their own story following a group discussion to gather and expand ideas. To extend the activity, have children come up with alternative story endings related to the theme. Divide the class into pairs, and have each pair of children complete a story based on the new ending.

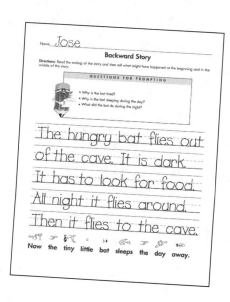

Descriptive Story

THEME	🐸 +S	🎩 +S	🐰 +S	🐤 +S	🌱 +S	🦋 +S
PAGE	38	55	73	90	107	124

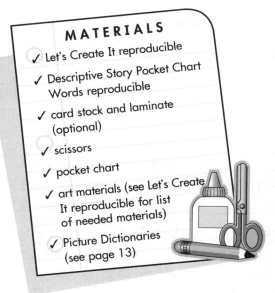

MATERIALS

✓ Let's Create It reproducible

✓ Descriptive Story Pocket Chart Words reproducible

✓ card stock and laminate (optional)

✓ scissors

✓ pocket chart

✓ art materials (see Let's Create It reproducible for list of needed materials)

✓ Picture Dictionaries (see page 13)

FOCUS

Children will use descriptive writing to write a sentence or story.

Make a copy of the Descriptive Story Pocket Chart Words from the page for the theme of study. As an option, copy the cards onto card stock and laminate them. Cut apart the word cards, and place them in a pocket chart. Copy a class set of the Let's Create It reproducible. Create a completed art sample following the directions on the reproducible. Review the vocabulary in the Picture Dictionary for the theme, and introduce the word cards in the pocket chart. Show children the completed sample, and review the steps they will need to follow to complete the project. Tell children that once they complete their project they are to write a sentence or story that goes with the project. Ask them to use the words from their Picture Dictionary and the word cards in the pocket chart to help them complete their writing. Have children work in a learning center to complete their project. When children have finished their project and writing, have them read their sentence or story to a partner or the whole class.

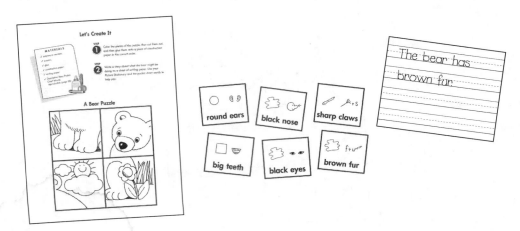

Shape Book

THEME	🐸 + s	🎩 + s	🐰 + s	🐤 + s	🪴 + s	🦋 + s
PAGE	39	57	74	91	108	125

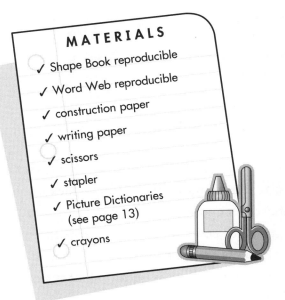

MATERIALS

✓ Shape Book reproducible
✓ Word Web reproducible
✓ construction paper
✓ writing paper
✓ scissors
✓ stapler
✓ Picture Dictionaries (see page 13)
✓ crayons

FOCUS

Children will practice informational writing.

Copy one class set of the Shape Book reproducible on construction paper. Copy one class set of the Word Web reproducible. As an option, laminate the Word Web reproducible for durability and place it in a learning center. Create a sample Shape Book to share with the class. Staple writing paper between a Shape Book reproducible and a blank piece of construction paper to create a booklet for each child. Demonstrate for children how to cut out the shape cover and by doing so create shaped writing paper and a back cover at the same time.

Have children review the vocabulary words in their Picture Dictionary for the appropriate theme. Tell children that they are to write about something they have learned from their theme of study. Review the words that appear on the Word Web reproducible. Invite children to share ideas about what they will write about in their shape book. Encourage them to use descriptive words in their story. Have children use their Picture Dictionary and the Word Web reproducible to help them spell the words they need to write sentences or stories in their shape book.

Invite children to color the cover of their book once their story is completed. Place the reproducibles at a learning center, and have small groups of children complete their books in the center with an adult. Younger writers may just write simple pattern sentences, while more advanced writers will combine ideas and thoughts into simple stories. Invite children to read their sentences or story to a partner or to the class.

Class Book

THEME	 +s	+s	+s	+s	+s	+s
PAGE	41	59	76	93	110	127

MATERIALS

✓ Class Book reproducible

✓ construction paper

✓ Picture Dictionaries (see page 13)

✓ crayons or markers

✓ bookbinding materials

FOCUS

Children will use adjectives in a series.

Copy a class set of the Class Book reproducible. Use construction paper to make a front and back cover for the class book. Show children the cover and the reproducible. Explain to children that they will each complete a page for the class book. Tell them that the completed book will be on display so everyone will have a chance to see their "work in print" and read what their classmates wrote. Discuss the cloze activity on the reproducible, and emphasize that children will complete the sentences by using words from their Picture Dictionary and words that appear around the room. Have children complete the cloze activity at a learning center or independently. Encourage them to use their Picture Dictionary for ideas. Have an adult do the actual writing for younger children. Tell these children to read back the sentence after an adult writes it. Have children illustrate their sentence. Assemble the completed pages, add the cover to the book, and then read the book to the class. Display the book in a prominent place, and invite children to read it during free time.

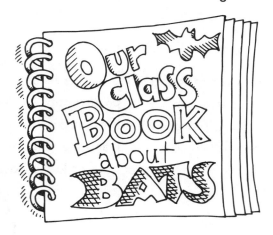

Sequence Story

THEME	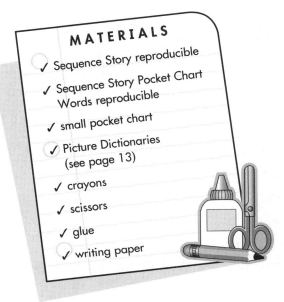 +S	+S	+S	+S	+S	+S
PAGE	42	60	77	94	111	128

MATERIALS

- ✓ Sequence Story reproducible
- ✓ Sequence Story Pocket Chart Words reproducible
- ✓ small pocket chart
- ✓ Picture Dictionaries (see page 13)
- ✓ crayons
- ✓ scissors
- ✓ glue
- ✓ writing paper

FOCUS

Children will write about a sequence of events over time.

Copy a class set of the Sequence Story reproducible. Create a sample Sequence Story to share when introducing the lesson. Make a copy of the Sequence Story Pocket Chart Words reproducible. Cut apart the word cards, and place them in a small pocket chart. Share these words with the class. Have them also review the words in their Picture Dictionary for the appropriate theme. Discuss with children the Sequence Story Prompt, which is listed on the section opener page. Show the class your Sequence Story sample. Explain to them that they will receive a series of pictures to color, cut out, and glue in proper sequence. Use the pictures from your sample as you discuss the sequence. Give each child a Sequence Story reproducible. Tell children to color, cut out, and glue the pictures in order on their reproducible. Then, have children use the Sequence Story Prompt to help them write a story about the theme on a piece of writing paper. Encourage children to use their Picture Dictionary and the pocket chart words to help them spell the words they need in order to write their sequence story. Invite volunteers to share their completed story.

Frogs  + s

The activities in this theme emphasize the use of describing words and the sequence of events. Additional vocabulary is introduced to promote descriptive and seasonal writing related to spring.

READ-ALOUDS

Frog
by Gail Gibbons
(HOLIDAY HOUSE)

A Frog in the Bog
by Karma Wilson
(MARGARET K. McELDERRY)

Frogs, Toads, and Turtles
by Diane L. Burns
(NORTH WORD PRESS)

From Tadpole to Frog
by Wendy Pfeffer
(HARPERCOLLINS)

Why Frogs Are Wet
by Judy Hawes
(HARPERCOLLINS)

PICTURE DICTIONARY WORDS

frog
tadpole
eggs
swim
water
gills
lungs
webbed feet
land
legs
tail
breathe

POCKET CHART WORDS

Descriptive Story	**Sequence Story**
slimy skin	cycle
bulging eyes	lays eggs
long sticky tongue	hatches
colored spots	pond
strong legs	amphibian
webbed feet	camouflage

EMPHASIZE THESE HAVE-TO WORDS IN THIS THEME:

under
(the dot is under the box)

 now
(/n/ + /ou/ I hit my finger with a hammer)

 use

 jump
(I can jump over the line)

 **swimming**
(swim + /ing/ king of the *ing*)

SENTENCE SQUARES SENTENCES

The tadpole can swim in water.
The frog has webbed feet to help it swim.
The frog lives in water and on land.
The frog lays eggs that hatch into tadpoles.

SEQUENCE STORY PROMPT

Explain how a tadpole turns into a frog.

Picture Dictionary Words

Directions: Read each word. Cut out the picture cards and glue them in your Picture Dictionary.

1. **frog**	2. **tadpole**	3. **eggs**
4. **swim**	5. **water**	6. **gills**
7. **lungs**	8. **webbed feet**	9. **land**
10. **legs**	11. **tail**	12. **breathe**

Pocket Chart Words

Descriptive Story (Use with Let's Create It on page 38)

sl + 👁 + 😊 sk+▫↙	⚾+j+👑 👁 👁	⌐ ✎+"E"
slimy skin	**bulging eyes**	**long sticky**
		😛
🖍 + ed	🙆 🚶↙	🦶 🦶
colored		
spots	**strong legs**	**webbed feet**

Sequence Story (Use with Sequence Story on page 42)

S + 👁 + k + l	l+"A"+s 🥚🥚	🥚 +s
cycle	**lays eggs**	**hatches**
🥔	⌣+m+f+"B"+"N"	K+m+◉+fl+j
pond	**amphibian**	**camouflage**

Rebus Writing • Spring © 2004 Creative Teaching Press

Name _____

Word Hunt

Directions: Use your Picture Dictionary to help you find the word that goes with each picture. Write the correct word below each picture. Complete the special sentence at the bottom of the page.

Rebus Writing • Spring © 2004 Creative Teaching Press

Secret Sentence Booklet

Directions: Write the correct word under each rebus picture.

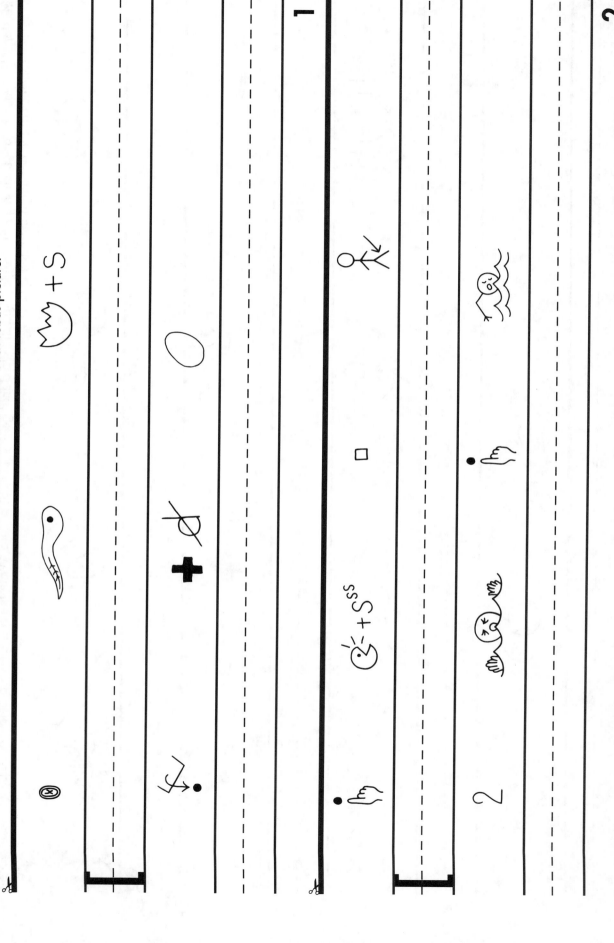

Rebus Writing • Spring © 2004 Creative Teaching Press

Secret Sentence Booklet

Directions: Write the correct word under each rebus picture.

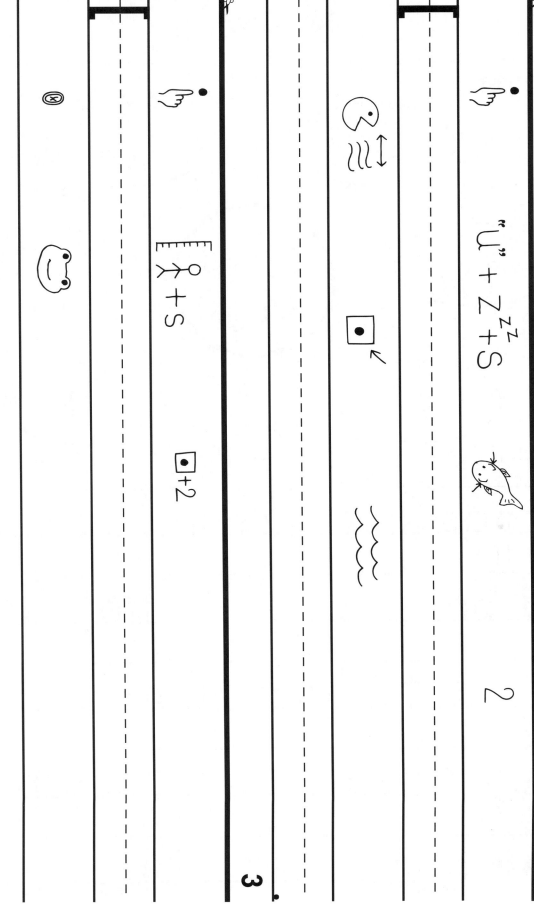

2

3

4

Rebus Writing • Spring © 2004 Creative Teaching Press

Bubble Writing

Directions: Write the correct word next to each bubble. Use these words to complete the sentences at the bottom of the page.

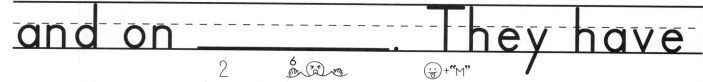

I Frogs can live in _____

and on _____. They have

_____ to help them _____.

They have _____ so

they can _____ on _____.

Rebus Writing • Spring © 2004 Creative Teaching Press

Connect a Sentence

Directions: Read the phrase in the center bubble. Add words from the connecting bubbles to the phrase to make a sentence. Use additional words to create more sentences. Write the sentences on a separate piece of paper.

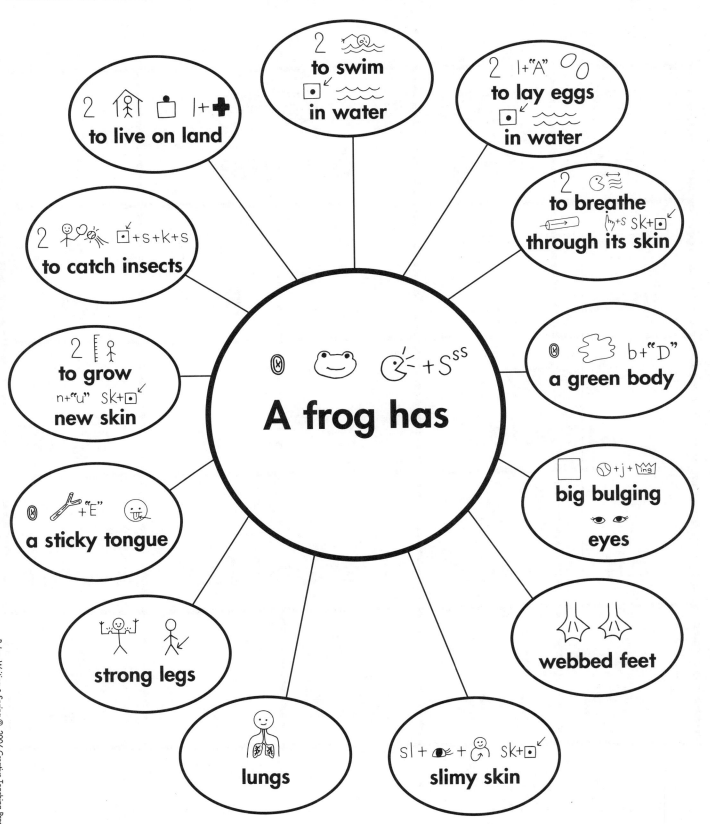

Rebus Writing • Spring © 2004 Creative Teaching Press

Sentence Squares

Directions: Read the word cards. Cut apart the cards and mix them up. Make sure that the words are face up. Use the word cards to make sentences.

The	frog	breathes	to
lives	in	lays	that	and
tadpole	has	it	eggs
on	swim	webbed feet	water
hatch	help	land	.	can

Rebus Writing • Spring © 2004 Creative Teaching Press

Sentence/Story Builder

Directions: Use the pictures to help you write a sentence or story that describes who, what, when, where, and why.

When	Who	Is Doing What	Where	Why
day	tree frog	puffs like a balloon	tree	noise

Rebus Writing • Spring © 2004 Creative Teaching Press

Story Box

Directions: Use the picture box ideas to write a story.

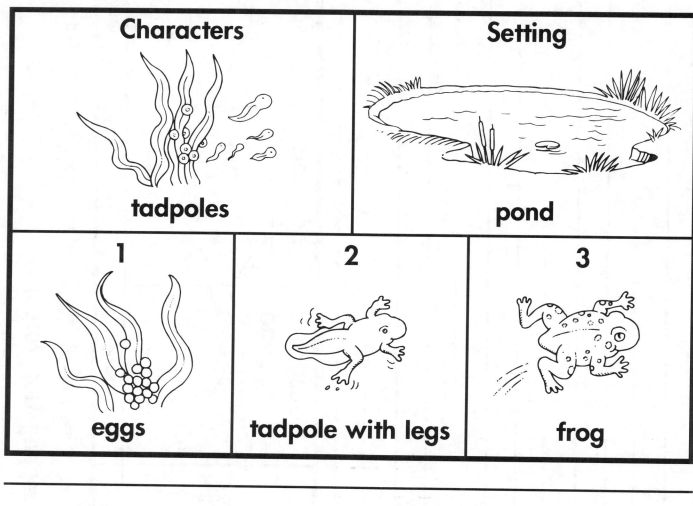

Rebus Writing • Spring © 2004 Creative Teaching Press

Name_____

Backward Story

Directions: Read the ending of the story and then tell what might have happened at the beginning and in the middle of the story.

QUESTIONS FOR PROMPTING

- What did the tadpole look like?
- Where did it live?
- How did it breathe?
- What did it eat?
- What happened to the tadpole as it got bigger?

_____

- - - - - - - - - - - - - - - - - - - -

_____

- - - - - - - - - - - - - - - - - - - -

_____

- - - - - - - - - - - - - - - - - - - -

_____

- - - - - - - - - - - - - - - - - - - -

_____

- - - - - - - - - - - - - - - - - - - -

Rebus Writing • Spring © 2004 Creative Teaching Press

Now the little tadpole has become a big

green frog.

Let's Create It

(Note to the teacher: Copy a class set of the Frog Pattern reproducible on heavy tagboard or card stock to create patterns for the frog's legs and eyes.)

MATERIALS

- ✓ small paper plate
- ✓ green and yellow construction paper
- ✓ scissors
- ✓ glue
- ✓ strips of red construction paper
- ✓ Picture Dictionary
- ✓ Descriptive Story Pocket Chart Words reproducible (page 28)

STEP 1

Fold a paper plate in half. Trace the frog leg pattern twice on a piece of green construction paper and cut out each leg. Then, glue the legs to the back flap of the paper plate. Trace each eye pattern twice on green and yellow construction paper and cut out the tracings. Glue the smaller yellow pieces onto the green pieces to make the eyes. Then, glue the eyes to the paper plate. Accordion-fold a 1" x 4" (2.5 cm x 10 cm) strip of red construction paper and glue one side of it to the inside of the paper plate.

STEP 2

Use your Picture Dictionary and the pocket chart words to help you write a sentence or story about your frog on a separate piece of paper.

Frog Pattern

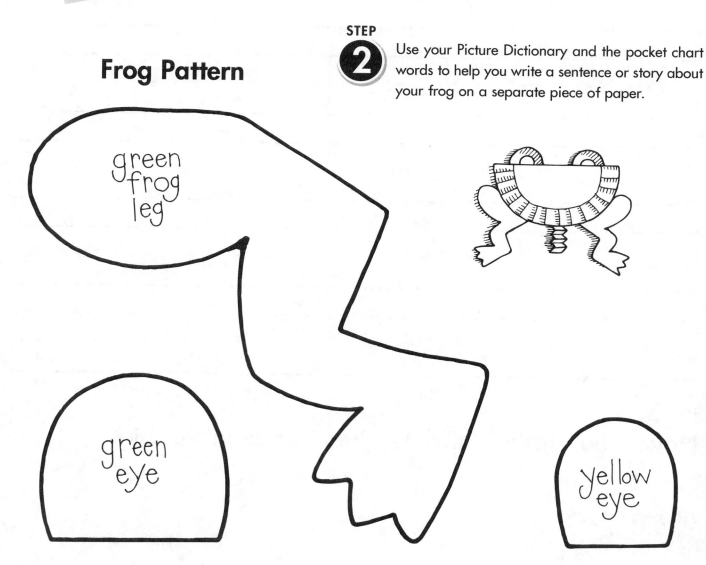

green frog leg

green eye

yellow eye

Rebus Writing • Spring © 2004 Creative Teaching Press

Shape Book

Directions: Color your cover. Cut out the cover and writing paper to create a shape book.

Word Web

Directions: Use the words on the word web to help you write a story.

Rebus Writing • Spring © 2004 Creative Teaching Press

Class Book

Directions: Use words from your Picture Dictionary and around the room to help you complete the sentences. Draw a picture to go with your sentences.

Once I was a little _Garl_ .

I had _toys_ and _dolls_ .

Then I grew into a big

adult. Now I can

bet and _fit_ .

By _'Alyssa_

Sequence Story

Directions: Color the pictures and cut them out. Glue the picture cards in order in the numbered boxes to show the sequence from an egg to a frog. Use the picture cards to write a story on another piece of paper. Use your Picture Dictionary and the Sequence Story Pocket Chart Words to help you.

1	2	3
4	5	6

Rebus Writing • Spring © 2004 Creative Teaching Press

Leprechauns  + s

Use this theme to promote imaginative writing. The activities in this theme emphasize the use of describing words and sequence of events. Additional vocabulary is introduced to promote descriptive writing and seasonal writing related to St. Patrick's Day.

READ-ALOUDS

Clever Tom and the Leprechaun: An Old Irish Story
by Linda Shute
(SCHOLASTIC)

Jack and the Leprechaun
by Katy Bratun
(RANDOM HOUSE)

Jamie O'Rourke and the Big Potato
by Tomie dePaola
(PUFFIN)

St. Patrick's Day in the Morning
by Jan Brett
(CLARION BOOKS)

PICTURE DICTIONARY WORDS

**leprechaun
shamrock
tiny
magical
tricks
joke
mischievous
disappear
chase
rainbow
pot of gold
good luck**

POCKET CHART WORDS

Descriptive Story	**Sequence Story**
shamrock hat	Ireland
orange beard	grassy fields
twinkle in his eye	end of the rainbow
friendly smile	magical powers
pointed ears	rich
green clothes	gold coins

EMPHASIZE THESE HAVE-TO WORDS IN THIS THEME:

did (I did it!)	**didn't**	**what** (what is in the box?)	**when** (when—day or night)	**from** (the dot fell from the shelf)

SENTENCE SQUARES SENTENCES

The leprechaun looks tiny and mischievous.
He likes to chase rainbows.
The leprechaun hunts for a pot of gold.
He has magical powers.
The leprechaun hides a pot of gold.

SEQUENCE STORY PROMPT

Tell a story about how the leprechaun finds a pot of gold.

Picture Dictionary Words

Directions: Read each word. Cut out the picture cards and glue them in your Picture Dictionary.

1. **leprechaun**	2.  **shamrock**	3.  **tiny**
4.  **magical**	5. **tricks**	6. $j + "O" + K$ **joke**
7. $m + s^{ss} + + "v" +$  **mischievous**	8. $d + s^{ss} + \circledR + "P" + $  **disappear**	9. **chase**
10.  **rainbow**	11. **pot of gold**	12. **good luck**

Rebus Writing • Spring © 2004 Creative Teaching Press

Pocket Chart Words

Descriptive Story (Use with Let's Create It on page 55)

shamrock hat	orange beard	twinkle in his eye
friendly smile	pointed ears	green clothes

Sequence Story (Use with Sequence Story on page 60)

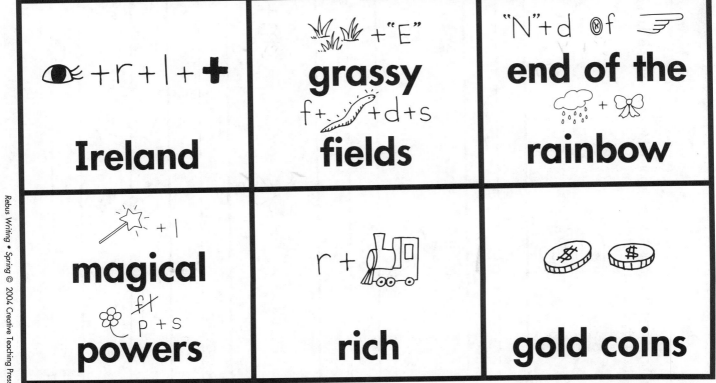

Ireland	grassy fields	end of the rainbow
magical powers	rich	gold coins

Rebus Writing • Spring © 2004 Creative Teaching Press

Name _____

Word Hunt

Directions: Use your Picture Dictionary to help you find the word that goes with each picture. Write the correct word below each picture. Complete the special sentence at the bottom of the page.

 j + "O" + K

 + tie + foot =

____

shamrock + "SS" + p

p + "SS" + S + (x) + "p" + ❤

____

 cloud + bow

m + "SS" + S + m

 pot

____

 hat

m + "SS" + S + leprechaun + "V" + faces

m + "SS" + S + leprechaun + "V" + faces

____

 finger + tie + foot

leprechaun ____

____

Secret Sentence Booklet

Directions: Write the correct word under each rebus picture.

        + − +

+ s   □• ←

dresses

1

m+s^{ss}+    +v+   + ◉◉+S

—

2   j+"O"+K+S +

play

2

Rebus Writing • Spring © 2004 Creative Teaching Press

Secret Sentence Booklet

Directions: Write the correct word under each rebus picture.

can

3

for

4

Name_____

Bubble Writing

Directions: Write the correct word next to each bubble. Use these words to complete the sentences at the bottom of the page.

Connect a Sentence

Directions: Read the phrase in the center bubble. Add words from the connecting bubbles to the phrase to make a sentence. Use additional words to create more sentences. Write the sentences on a separate piece of paper.

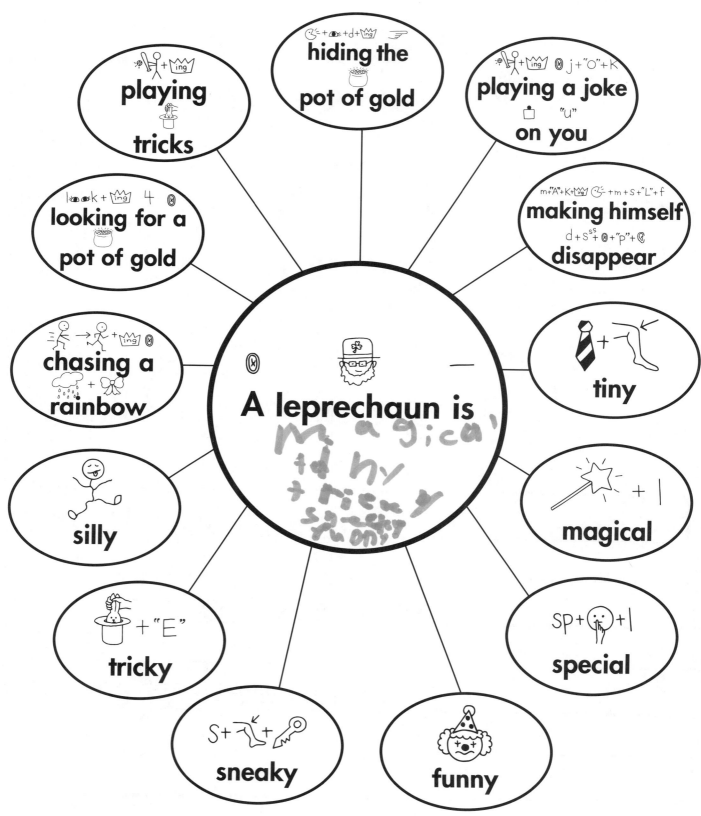

Rebus Writing • Spring © 2004 Creative Teaching Press

Sentence Squares

Directions: Read the word cards. Cut apart the cards and mix them up. Make sure that the words are face up. Use the word cards to make sentences.

He	powers	rainbows	The
pot of gold	a	hunts	.
looks	leprechaun	and	likes
chase	hides	tiny	for	to
magical	mischievous	has	

Sentence/Story Builder

Directions: Use the pictures to help you write a sentence or story that describes who, what, when, where, and why.

When	Who	Is Doing What	Where	Why
sunny day	leprechaun	looking for magic shamrocks	meadow	turn into gold

Rebus Writing • Spring © 2004 Creative Teaching Press

Story Box

Directions: Use the picture box ideas to write a story.

Character	Setting
leprechaun	outside

1	2	3
raining	rainbow	pot of gold

Once Upon a Time
a leprechaun
sat by a
pot of. gold

Backward Story

Directions: Read the ending of the story and then tell what might have happened at the beginning and in the middle of the story.

QUESTIONS FOR PROMPTING
• Where was the leprechaun?
• What was this leprechaun like?
• Why did he want gold?
• Where did he find the pot of gold?
• Why did he hide it?
• Where did he hide it?

The tiny little leprechaun knew that no one

would ever find his pot of gold.

Rebus Writing • Spring © 2004 Creative Teaching Press

Let's Create It

(Note to the teacher: Copy a class set of the Leprechaun Face reproducible on white construction paper.)

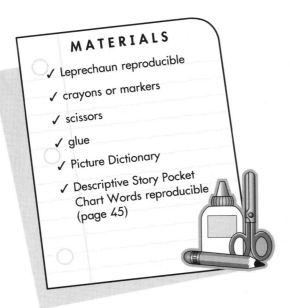

MATERIALS

✓ Leprechaun reproducible

✓ crayons or markers

✓ scissors

✓ glue

✓ Picture Dictionary

✓ Descriptive Story Pocket Chart Words reproducible (page 45)

STEP 1

Color the leprechaun face, hat, and nose. Cut out each piece. Fold the hat and nose on the dotted lines. Keep the flap of the hat folded up, and glue the hat to the leprechaun face. Put glue on the folded flap of the nose, and place the nose on the face.

STEP 2

Use your Picture Dictionary and the pocket chart words to help you write a sentence or story about your leprechaun on a separate piece of paper.

Leprechaun Face

Rebus Writing • Spring © 2004 Creative Teaching Press

Shape Book

Directions: Color your cover. Cut out the cover and writing paper to create a shape book.

Word Web

Directions: Use the words on the word web to help you write a story.

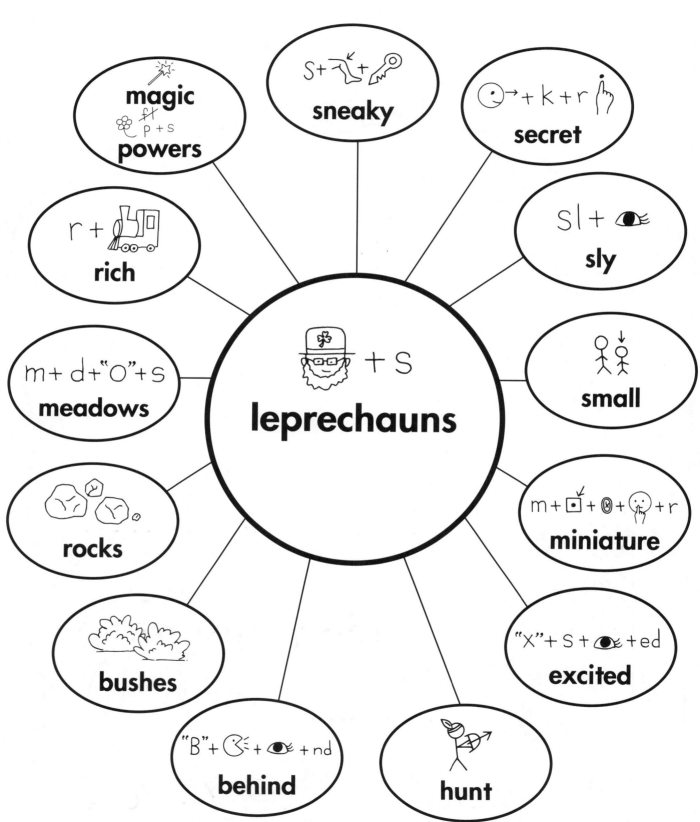

Rebus Writing • Spring © 2004 Creative Teaching Press

Class Book

Directions: Use words from your Picture Dictionary and around the room to help you complete the sentences. Draw a picture to go with your sentences.

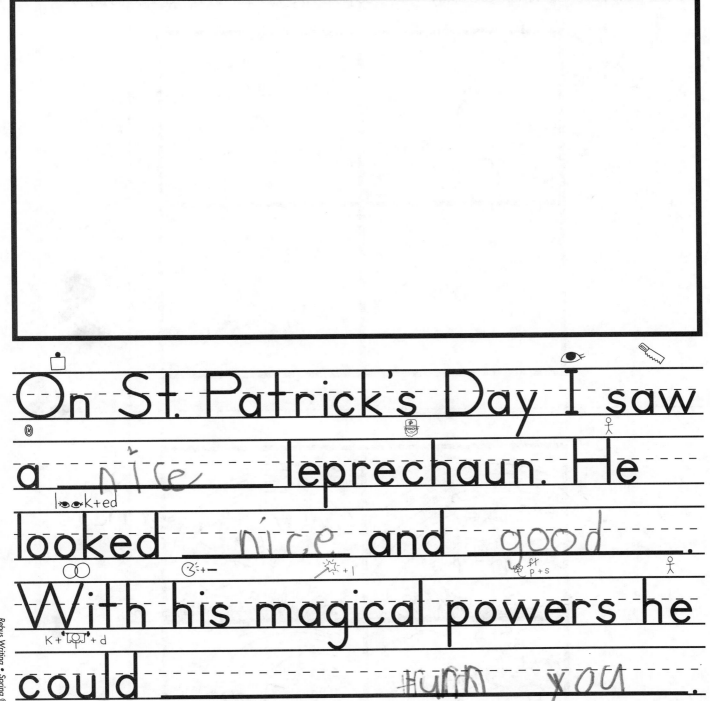

On St. Patrick's Day I saw
a _nice_ leprechaun. He
looked _nice_ and _good_.
With his magical powers he
could _turn you_.

By _Alyssa_

Rebus Writing • Spring © 2004 Creative Teaching Press

Sequence Story

Directions: Color the pictures and cut them out. Glue the picture cards in order in the numbered boxes to show the sequence of a leprechaun finding a pot of gold. Use the picture cards to write a story on another piece of paper. Use your Picture Dictionary and the Sequence Story Pocket Chart Words to help you.

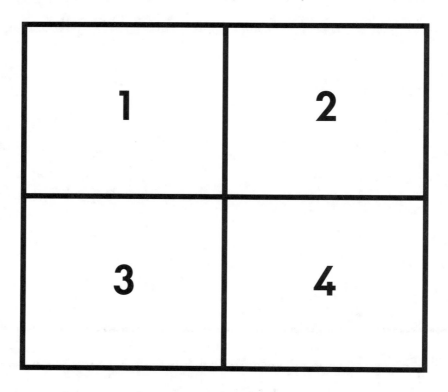

Rabbits

The activities in this theme emphasize the use of describing words and facts about how rabbits live and protect themselves. Additional vocabulary is introduced to promote descriptive writing and seasonal writing related to spring.

READ-ALOUDS

Life Cycle of a Rabbit
by Lisa Trumbauer
(PEBBLE BOOKS)

Rabbits and Hares
by Diane Swanson
(GARETH STEVENS)

Rabbits, Rabbits, & More Rabbits!
by Gail Gibbons
(HOLIDAY HOUSE)

The Runaway Bunny
by Margaret Wise Brown
(HARPERTROPHY)

The Velveteen Rabbit
by Margery Williams
(ATHENEUM)

PICTURE DICTIONARY WORDS

rabbit
whiskers
soft
long ears
strong legs
jump
hop
burrow
hearing
smell
enemies
protect

POCKET CHART WORDS

Descriptive Story	**Sequence Story**
floppy ears	camouflage
beady little eyes	surroundings
small black nose	hide
long whiskers	communicate
sharp teeth	danger
fluffy tail	thumping ground

EMPHASIZE THESE HAVE-TO WORDS IN THIS THEME:

about
(/u/ the belly button sound + /b/ + out)

away
(/u/ the belly button sound + a one-way street sign)

pull

long

how
(/h/ breathe out + /ou/ I hit my thumb with a hammer)

SENTENCE SQUARES SENTENCES

Rabbits have soft fur and strong legs.
They have good ears to hear enemies.
Rabbits like to run, hop, and eat grass.
Rabbits have strong legs to run from enemies.
They like to hop and jump.

SEQUENCE STORY PROMPT

Tell a story about how a mother rabbit protects her babies.

Picture Dictionary Words

Directions: Read each word. Cut out the picture cards and glue them in your Picture Dictionary.

1. rabbit	2. whiskers	3. soft
4. long ears	**5. strong legs**	**6. jump**
7. hop	8. $b + ur^{rr} + "o"$ **burrow**	9. **hearing**
10. $s + m + "L"$ **smell**	11. $"N" + \oslash + \text{(man)} + s$ **enemies**	12. **protect**

Rebus Writing • Spring © 2004 Creative Teaching Press

Pocket Chart Words

Descriptive Story (Use with Let's Create It on page 73)

fl + "P" 👂👂 **floppy ears**	"B" + "D" ▫ **beady little** 👁 👁 **eyes**	**small black** **nose**
long **whiskers**	 **sharp teeth**	 **fluffy tail**

Sequence Story (Use with Sequence Story on page 77)

K + m + ⊗ + fl + j **camouflage**	S + ur^rr + ○ + 👑ing + s **surroundings**	+👁+d **hide**
K + ⊗ + m + 👻°° + ⚡ + K + 8 **communicate**	☀️☁️ + n + j + er^rr **danger**	✋ + p + 👑ing **thumping** g + ○ **ground**

Rebus Writing • Spring © 2004 Creative Teaching Press

Word Hunt

Directions: Use your Picture Dictionary to help you find the word that goes with each picture. Write the correct word below each picture. Complete the special sentence at the bottom of the page.

 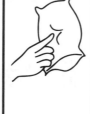 

$\boxed{}$ $\odot\odot$ ⌣ + ⌣ + ing

- -

"N" + + 🙂 + S       b + ur^{r} + "o"

- -

S + m + "L"      ⌣ + S^{ss} $\boxed{}$

- -

$\boxed{}$ •

Secret Sentence Booklet

Directions: Write the correct word under each rebus picture.

 +S   "R"   "q"+t   +

_____

   f + urrrr

 "A"

 @ 6   +

Rebus Writing • Spring © 2004 Creative Teaching Press

Secret Sentence Booklet

Directions: Write the correct word under each rebus picture.

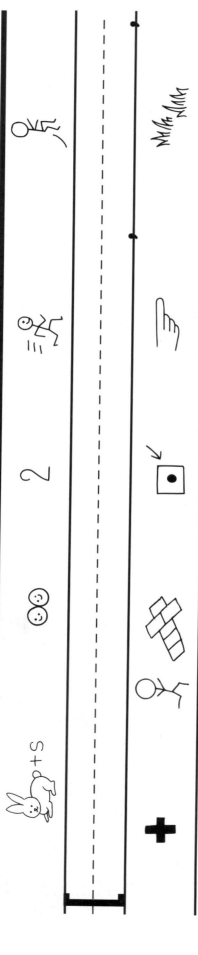

grass

3

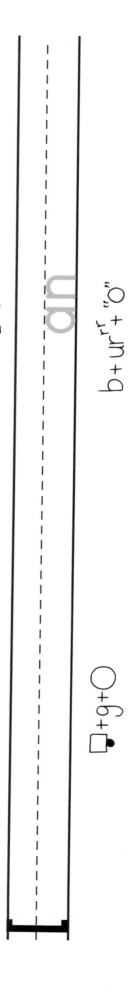

an

underground

4

Rebus Writing • Spring © 2004 Creative Teaching Press

Bubble Writing

Directions: Write the correct word next to each bubble. Use these words to complete the sentences at the bottom of the page.

Connect a Sentence

Directions: Read the phrase in the center bubble. Add words from the connecting bubbles to the phrase to make a sentence. Use additional words to create more sentences. Write the sentences on a separate piece of paper.

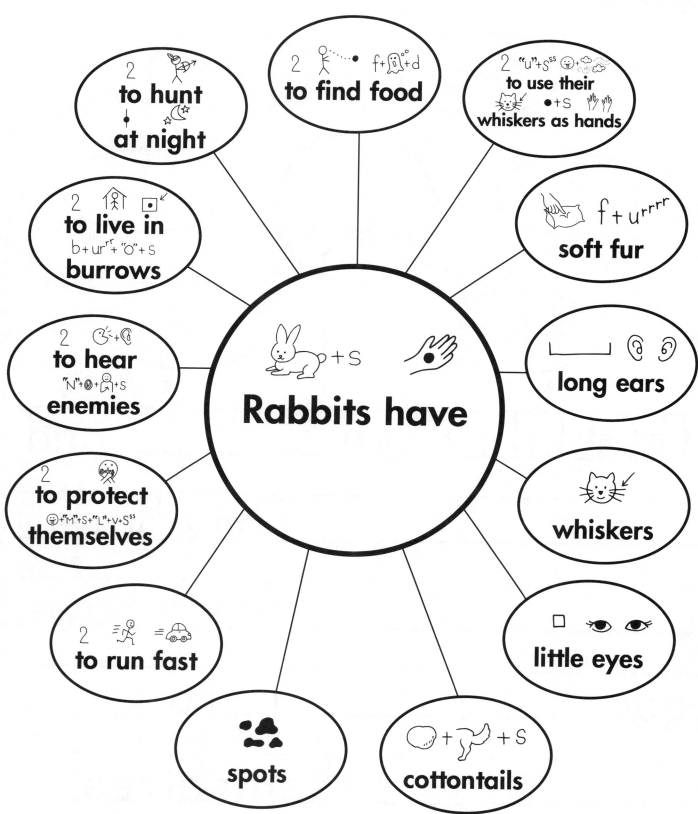

Rebus Writing • Spring © 2004 Creative Teaching Press

Sentence Squares

Directions: Read the word cards. Cut apart the cards and mix them up. Make sure that the words are face up. Use the word cards to make sentences.

They	strong	like	hop	hear
Rabbits		enemies		soft
run	have	to	fur	jump
ears	eat	grass	and	good
legs	from	.		

Rebus Writing • Spring © 2004 Creative Teaching Press

Sentence/Story Builder

Directions: Use the pictures to help you write a sentence or story that describes **who, what, when, where,** and **why.**

When	Who	Is Doing What	Where	Why
night	jack rabbits	hunt	woods	food

Story Box

Directions: Use the picture box ideas to write a story.

Characters

friends

Setting

classroom

1 dyeing eggs

2 hiding eyes

3 hunting for eggs

I had a friends we were hunting for eggs

Backward Story

Directions: Read the ending of the story and then tell what might have happened at the beginning and in the middle of the story.

QUESTIONS FOR PROMPTING

- What did the little rabbit look like?
- Where was the rabbit before going into the burrow?
- Why was the rabbit so tired?
- What had the rabbit been doing?

Then   the   little   rabbit   snuggled   up   in   his

burrow   and   went   to   sleep.

Rebus Writing • Spring © 2004 Creative Teaching Press

Let's Create It

MATERIALS

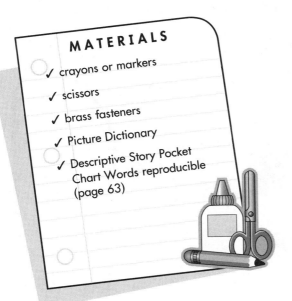

- ✓ crayons or markers
- ✓ scissors
- ✓ brass fasteners
- ✓ Picture Dictionary
- ✓ Descriptive Story Pocket Chart Words reproducible (page 63)

STEP 1
Color the rabbit. Cut out the pieces, and place the bunny on top of the circle so the dots meet. Place a brass fastener through both dots. Turn and read.

STEP 2
Use your Picture Dictionary and the pocket chart words to help you write a story about your rabbit on a separate piece of paper.

Rabbit Wheel

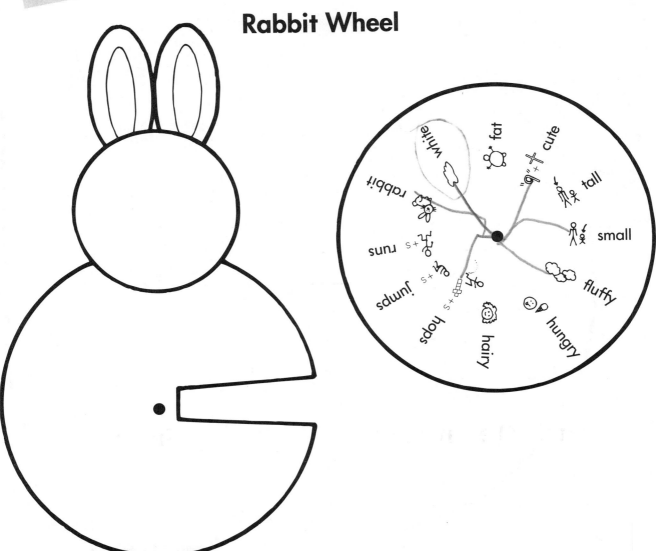

Shape Book

Directions: Color your cover. Cut out the cover and writing paper to create a shape book.

Rebus Writing • Spring © 2004 Creative Teaching Press

Word Web

Directions: Use the words on the word web to help you write a story.

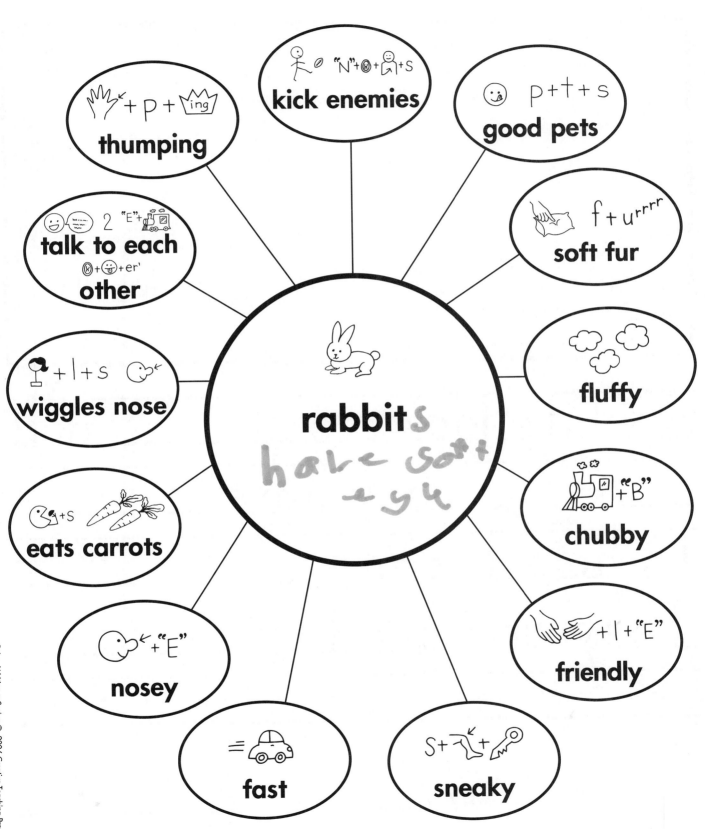

rabbit**s** *have soft*
+ y 4

Class Book

Directions: Use words from your Picture Dictionary and around the room to help you complete the sentences. Draw a picture to go with your sentences.

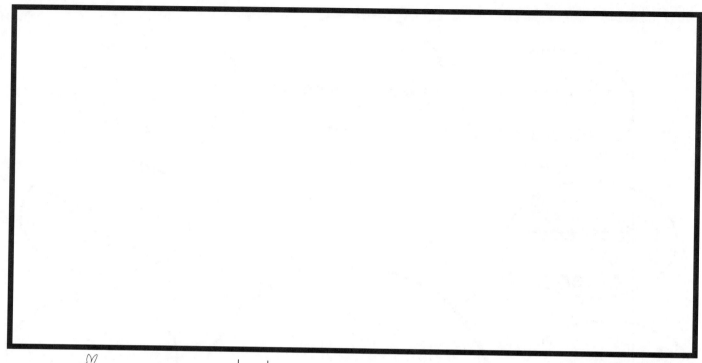

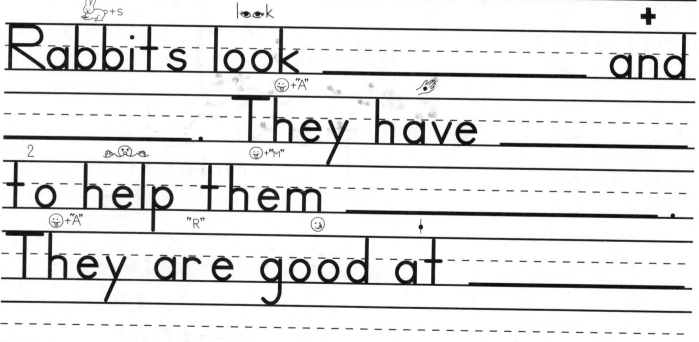

Rabbits look _____ and

_____. They have _____

to help them _____.

They are good at _____

_____.

By _____

Rebus Writing • Spring © 2004 Creative Teaching Press

Sequence Story

Directions: Color the pictures and cut them out. Glue the picture cards in order in the numbered boxes to show the sequence of how a mother rabbit protects her babies. Use the picture cards to write a story on another piece of paper. Use your Picture Dictionary and the Sequence Story Pocket Chart Words to help you.

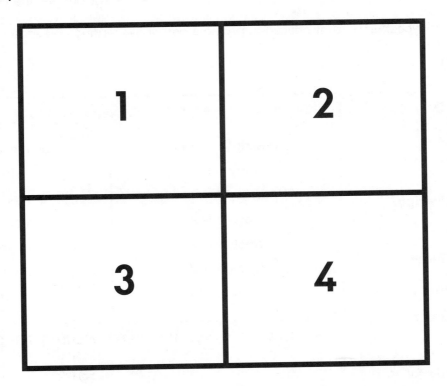

Chicks

 + s

The activities in this theme emphasize the use of describing words and the life cycle of a chicken. Additional vocabulary is introduced to promote descriptive writing and seasonal writing related to seasons.

READ-ALOUDS

Chick & Chickens
by Gail Gibbons
(HOLIDAY HOUSE)

The Chicken or the Egg?
by Allan Fowler
(CHILDREN'S PRESS)

From Chick to Chicken
by Jillian Powell
(RAINTREE/STECK VAUGHN)

From Egg to Chicken
by Gerald Legg
(FRANKLIN WATTS)

Something Wonderful
by Jenny Nimmo
(HARCOURT)

PICTURE DICTIONARY WORDS

**chick
hatches
brooding
warm
cracks
shell
milk tooth
comb
beak
wattle
hen
rooster**

POCKET CHART WORDS

Descriptive Story	Sequence Story
furry body	farm
sharp teeth	incubator
wobbly feet	three weeks
small wings	yolk
feathery tail	food sack
funny wattle	cycle

EMPHASIZE THESE HAVE-TO WORDS IN THIS THEME:

keep **her** **out** **thing**

(/th/ stick out your tongue sound + /ing/ king of the *ing*)

something

(/s/ + /u/ the belly button sound + /m/ + thing)

SENTENCE SQUARES SENTENCES

Chicks have a comb, beak, wattle, and feathers.
Chicks have to peck at seeds.
They like to scratch and strut.
Chicks have wings and a yellow beak.
They eat worms and seeds.

SEQUENCE STORY PROMPT

Write a story about the life cycle of a chick.

Picture Dictionary Words

Directions: Read each word. Cut out the picture cards and glue them in your Picture Dictionary.

1.  **chick**	2. 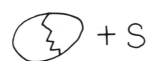 **hatches**	3. br+ 👻 +d+ ing **brooding**
4. W+ 🚶 **warm**	5. 🥚 +S **cracks**	6. 😶 + " L " **shell**
7.  milk + 😊 **milk tooth**	8. **comb**	9. 🐤 **beak**
10.  **wattle**	11. + " N " **hen**	12. r+ 👻 +st+err **rooster**

Pocket Chart Words

Descriptive Story (Use with Let's Create It on page 90)

f + u^{rrrr} + "E" b + "D"		w + b + l + "E"
furry body	**sharp teeth**	**wobbly feet**
w + ⬡ing + s	+ "E"	
small wings	**feathery tail**	**funny wattle**

Sequence Story (Use with Sequence Story on page 94)

f +	+ "q" + b + "A" + t + er^{rr}	3 + k + s
farm	**incubator**	**three weeks**
	f + + d S + k	S + + k + l
yolk	**food sack**	**cycle**

Rebus Writing • Spring © 2004 Creative Teaching Press

Name _____

Word Hunt

Directions: Use your Picture Dictionary to help you find the word that goes with each picture. Write the correct word below each picture. Complete the special sentence at the bottom of the page.

br+  +d+ ing   + " N "   + " L "

_____   _____   _____

milk +      ⦀(comb)   w+ (stick figure)

_____   _____   _____

r+ (ghost)+st+err   (chick)   +s   (egg)

_____   _____   _____

br+ (ghost)+d+ ing   (key)+p+s   (wing)   (chick)   w+ (stick figure)

_____   _____   _____

keeps

Rebus Writing • Spring © 2004 Creative Teaching Press

Secret Sentence Booklet

Directions: Write the correct word under each rebus picture.

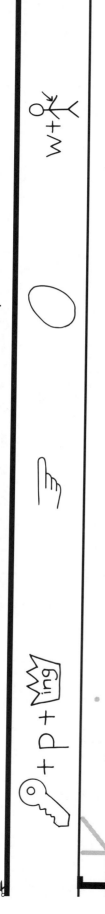

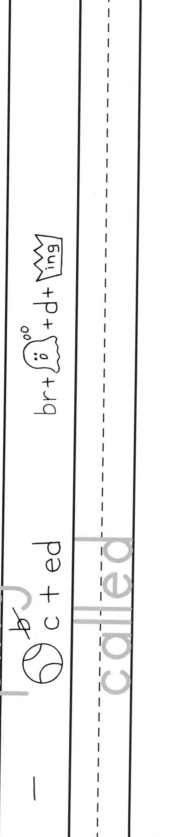

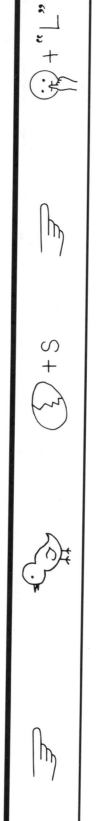

key + p + ing

I Keeping

b c + ed

br + d + ing

called

1

S

with

milk +

2

Rebus Writing • Spring © 2004 Creative Teaching Press

Secret Sentence Booklet

Directions: Write the correct word under each rebus picture.

2

b + "A" + B"   —

baby +   f + u"r"r"r" + "E"

furry

3

          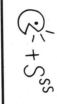

      + S^{ss}   ⊗   ⫿⫿⫿⫿

4

⊗   +   ⊗

Bubble Writing

Directions: Write the correct word next to each bubble. Use these words to complete the sentences at the bottom of the page.

Rebus Writing • Spring © 2004 Creative Teaching Press

Connect a Sentence

Directions: Read the phrase in the center bubble. Add words from the connecting bubbles to the phrase to make a sentence. Use additional words to create more sentences. Write the sentences on a separate piece of paper.

Sentence Squares

Directions: Read the word cards. Cut apart the cards and mix them up. Make sure that the words are face up. Use the word cards to make sentences.

Chicks	yellow	beak	at	have
to	wings	peck	feathers	
seeds	They	a	comb	scratch
eat	strut	and	worms	like
wattle	.			

Rebus Writing • Spring © 2004 Creative Teaching Press

Sentence/Story Builder

Directions: Use the pictures to help you write a sentence or story that describes **who, what, when, where,** and **why.**

When	Who	Is Doing What	Where	Why
today	chick	egg cracked open	incubator	hatched

Story Box

Directions: Use the picture box ideas to write a story.

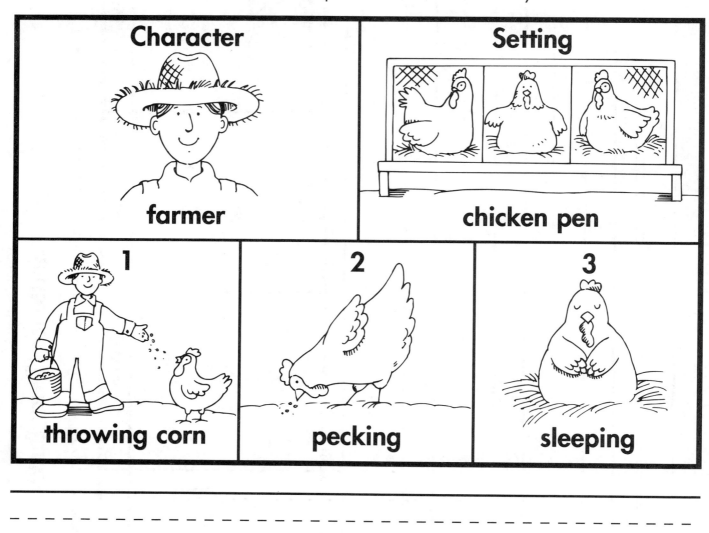

Character

farmer

Setting

chicken pen

1 throwing corn

2 pecking

3 sleeping

Name_____

Backward Story

Directions: Read the ending of the story and then tell what might have happened at the beginning and in the middle of the story.

QUESTIONS FOR PROMPTING

- Where were the hen and baby chicks?
- What were they doing?
- Why was the mother hen proud of her baby chicks?

_____

- -

_____

- -

_____

- -

_____

- -

_____

- -

_____

- -

_____

       +

Then   the   mother   hen   lifted   her   wing   and

hugged   her   baby   chicks.

Rebus Writing • Spring © 2004 Creative Teaching Press

Let's Create It

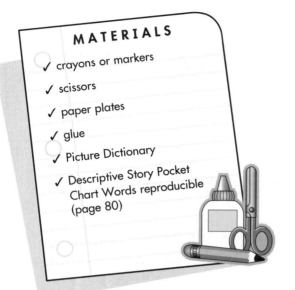

STEP 1

Cut out a circle from white construction paper to make a chick's head. Color the parts of a chick. Cut out the pieces, and glue them to the circle cutout and a paper plate as shown in the completed picture.

STEP 2

Use your Picture Dictionary and the pocket chart words to help you write a story about your chick on a separate piece of paper.

Chick

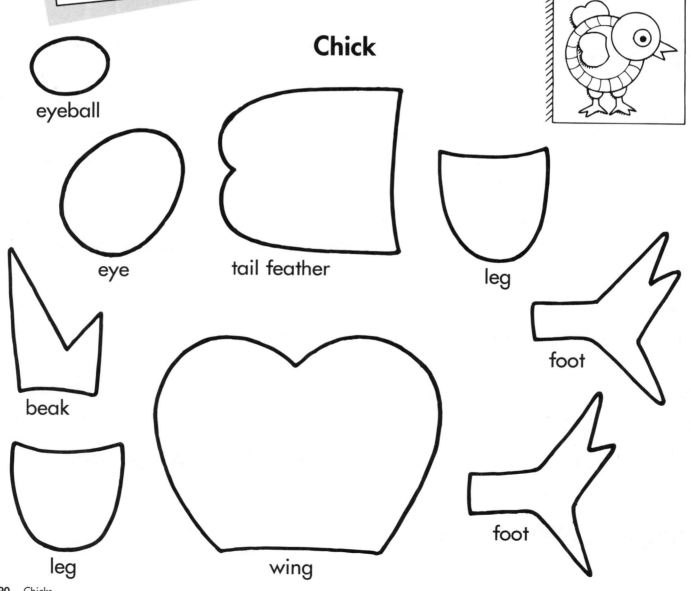

eyeball

eye

tail feather

leg

beak

foot

leg

wing

foot

Rebus Writing • Spring © 2004 Creative Teaching Press

Shape Book

Directions: Color your cover. Cut out the cover and writing paper to create a shape book.

Rebus Writing • Spring © 2004 Creative Teaching Press

Word Web

Directions: Use the words on the word web to help you write a story.

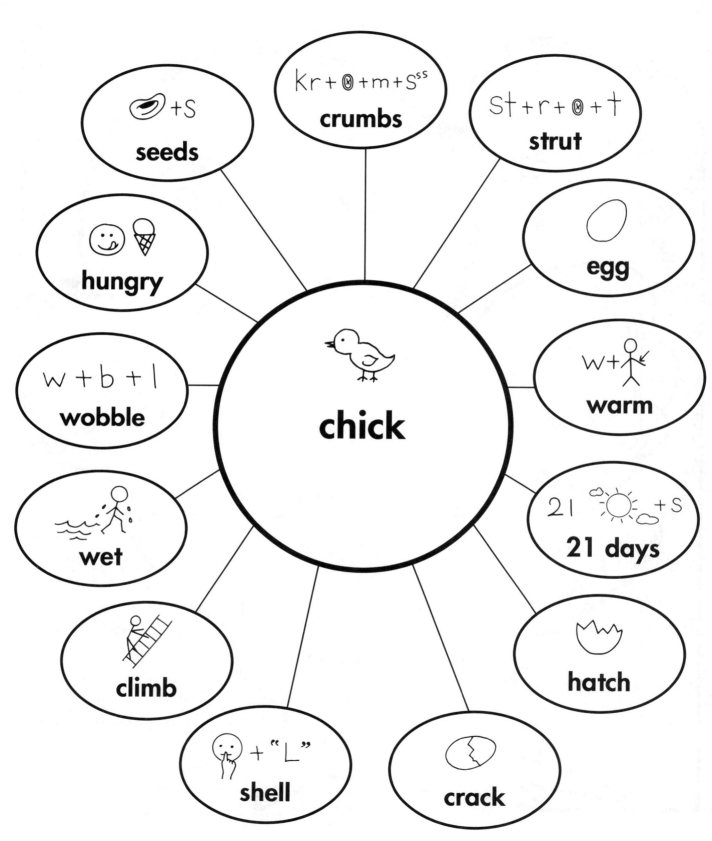

Rebus Writing • Spring © 2004 Creative Teaching Press

Class Book

Directions: Use words from your Picture Dictionary and around the room to help you complete the sentences. Draw a picture to go with your sentences.

1. After 2 days, the _____ hatches. It is _____ and _____. When the baby chick's feathers dry, it looks _____. Then the chick _____.

By _____

Rebus Writing • Spring © 2004 Creative Teaching Press

Sequence Story

Directions: Color the pictures and cut them out. Glue the picture cards in order in the numbered boxes to show the sequence of the chick's life cycle. Use the picture cards to write a story on another piece of paper. Use your Picture Dictionary and the Sequence Story Pocket Chart Words to help you.

1	**2**	**3**
4	**5**	**6**

Rebus Writing • Spring © 2004 Creative Teaching Press

Plants

+ s

The activities in this theme emphasize the use of describing words and the sequence of events. Additional vocabulary is introduced to promote descriptive and seasonal writing related to the life cycle of a plant.

READ-ALOUDS

From Seed to Plant
by Gail Gibbons
(HOLIDAY HOUSE)

How a Seed Grows
by Helene J. Jordan
(HARPERTROPHY)

The Magic School Bus Plants Seeds: A Book About How Living Things Grow
by Joanna Cole
(SCHOLASTIC)

Oh Say Can You Seed?: All About Flowering Plants
by Aristides Ruiz
(RANDOM HOUSE)

A Seed Grows: My First Look at a Plant's Life Cycle
(KIDS CAN PRESS)

PICTURE DICTIONARY WORDS

plant
seed
root
sprout
stem
flower
leaves
sunlight
water
air
dirt
grow

POCKET CHART WORDS

Descriptive Story	**Sequence Story**
hairy roots	hard coat
long stem	cracks open
tiny bud	soaks up
green leaves	minerals
beautiful	makes food
blossom	makes seeds

EMPHASIZE THESE HAVE-TO WORDS IN THIS THEME:

need
(knee +/d/)

also
(ball without the "b" + sew with a needle and thread)

soon
(/s/ + /oo/ the ghost sound + /n/)

for

push
(/p/ + /sh/ finger over lips)

SENTENCE SQUARES SENTENCES

The plant has roots.
The plant needs sunlight.
It needs water and air.
It sprouts through the dirt.
The plant has leaves to make food.
It has a flower to make new seeds.

SEQUENCE STORY PROMPT

Write a story about the life cycle of a plant.

Picture Dictionary Words

Directions: Read each word. Cut out the picture cards and glue them in your Picture Dictionary.

1. **plant**	2. **seed**	3. **root**
4. **sprout**	5. **stem**	6. **flower**
7. **leaves**	8. **sunlight**	9. **water**
10. **air**	11. **dirt**	12. **grow**

Rebus Writing • Spring © 2004 Creative Teaching Press

Pocket Chart Words

Descriptive Story (Use with Let's Create It on page 107)

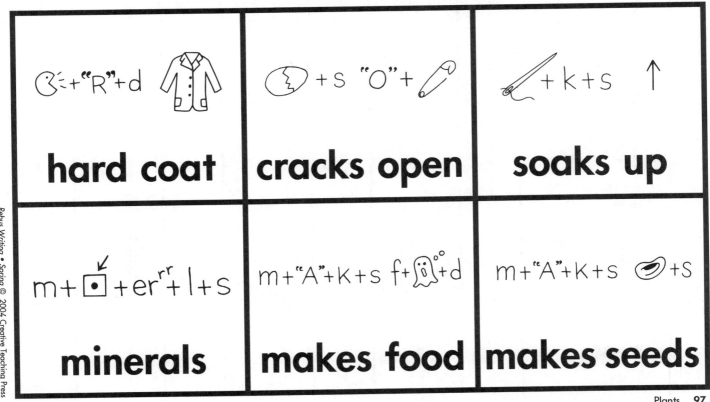

hairy roots	long stem	tiny bud
green leaves	beautiful	blossom

Sequence Story (Use with Sequence Story on page 111)

hard coat	cracks open	soaks up
minerals	makes food	makes seeds

Rebus Writing • Spring © 2004 Creative Teaching Press

Name _____

Word Hunt

Directions: Use your Picture Dictionary to help you find the word that goes with each picture. Write the correct word below each picture. Complete the special sentence at the bottom of the page.

Secret Sentence Booklet

Directions: Write the correct word under each rebus picture.

☀ + 💡   ☂ + d + s

2   📏

🌱 + d + s

1

☝•

⚾🪡 +   👣 + d + s   〰

also

➕   ☁🌧

2   📏

Rebus Writing • Spring © 2004 Creative Teaching Press

2

Secret Sentence Booklet

Directions: Write the correct word under each rebus picture.

  "U"   ⊗

When

 🔆+s E🔆+s

2

 s+🐱+n 🌱+s 🌱+s

3

↑ 🔺 ☝ 👣

4

Rebus Writing • Spring © 2004 Creative Teaching Press

Bubble Writing

Directions: Write the correct word next to each bubble. Use these words to complete the sentences at the bottom of the page.

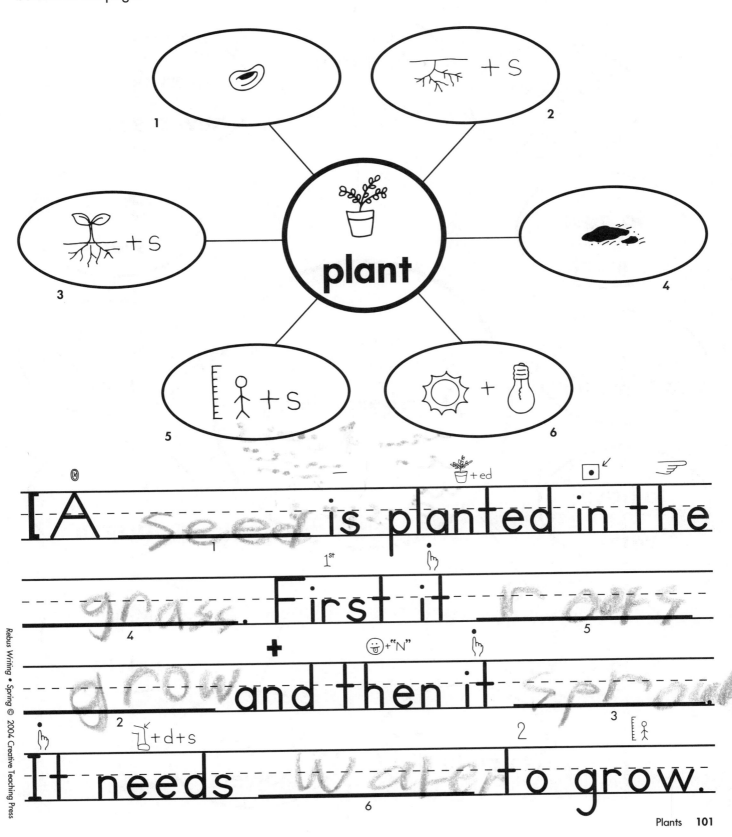

I A _seed_ is planted in the

grass. First it r oots

grow and then it sprouts

It needs water to grow.

Connect a Sentence

Directions: Read the phrase in the center bubble. Add words from the connecting bubbles to the phrase to make a sentence. Use additional words to create more sentences. Write the sentences on a separate piece of paper.

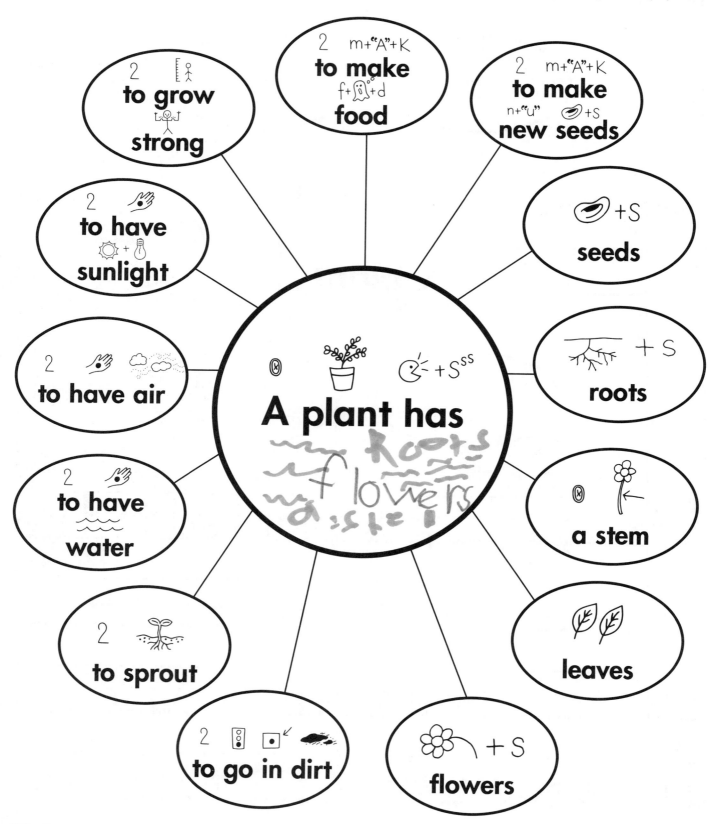

Rebus Writing • Spring © 2004 Creative Teaching Press

Sentence Squares

Directions: Read the word cards. Cut apart the cards and mix them up. Make sure that the words are face up. Use the word cards to make sentences.

a	plant	the	It	to
air	has	needs	make	leaves
through	water		sunlight	
and	food	dirt	seeds	sprouts
flower	roots	The	.	new

Rebus Writing • Spring © 2004 Creative Teaching Press

Sentence/Story Builder

Directions: Use the pictures to help you write a sentence or story that describes **who, what, when, where,** and **why.**

When	Who	Is Doing What	Where	Why
one day	my friend and I	planted a seed	garden	flower

Name_____

Story Box

Directions: Use the picture box ideas to write a story.

Characters

friends

Setting

school garden

1 digging and planting

2 watering

3 giving flowers

I had

Rebus Writing • Spring © 2004 Creative Teaching Press

Backward Story

Directions: Read the ending of the story and then tell what might have happened at the beginning and in the middle of the story.

QUESTIONS FOR PROMPTING

- Where did the flower come from?
- Who planted it?
- What made the flower grow?

Then I picked that special flower and

gave it to my grandmother.

Let's Create It

(Note to the teacher: Copy a class set of the Flower Pattern reproducible on white construction paper.)

MATERIALS

- ✓ white construction paper
- ✓ crayons or markers
- ✓ scissors
- ✓ glue
- ✓ Picture Dictionary
- ✓ Descriptive Story Pocket Chart Words reproducible (page 97)

STEP 1

Color the seed, stem, and flower. Cut out the pieces. Glue the flower to the top of the stem. Fold the stem on the dotted lines. Glue the folded flower on the bottom back of the seed.

STEP 2

Use your Picture Dictionary and the pocket chart words to help you write a sentence or story about your flower on a separate piece of paper.

Flower Pattern

Shape Book

Directions: Color your cover. Cut out the cover and writing paper to create a shape book.

Word Web

Directions: Use the words on the word web to help you write a story.

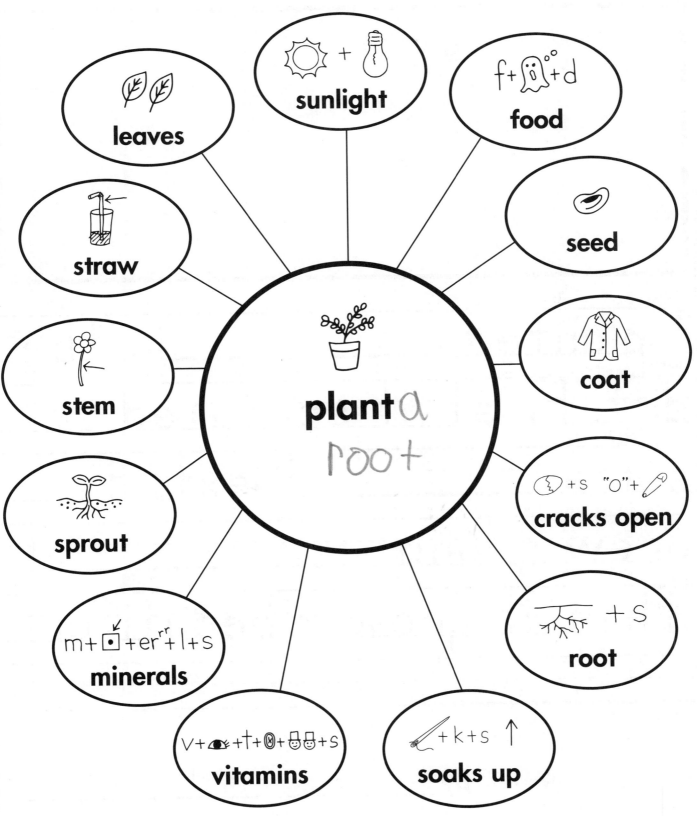

Rebus Writing • Spring © 2004 Creative Teaching Press

Class Book

Directions: Use words from your Picture Dictionary and around the room to help you complete the sentences. Draw a picture to go with your sentences.

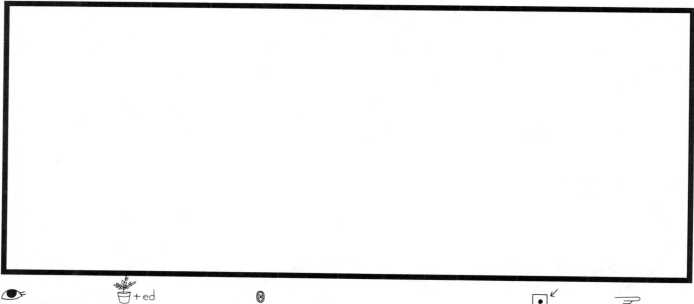

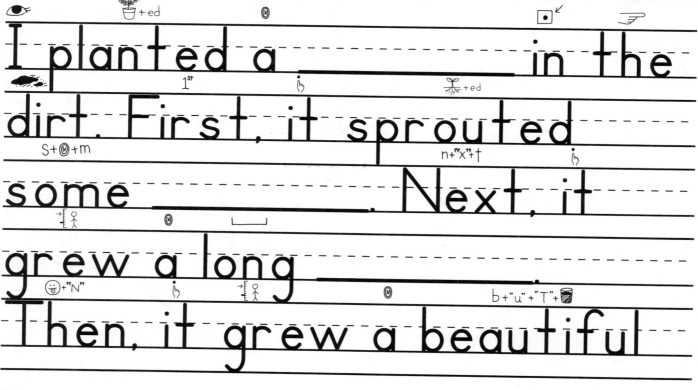

I planted a _____ in the dirt. First, it sprouted some _____. Next, it grew a long _____. Then, it grew a beautiful _____.

By _____

Rebus Writing • Spring © 2004 Creative Teaching Press

Sequence Story

Directions: Color the pictures and cut them out. Glue the picture cards in order in the numbered boxes to show the life cycle of a plant. Use the picture cards to write a story on another piece of paper. Use your Picture Dictionary and the Sequence Story Pocket Chart Words to help you.

1	2	3
4	5	6

- -

Butterflies

The activities in this theme emphasize describing words and the life cycle of a butterfly. Additional vocabulary is introduced to promote descriptive writing and drawing conclusions.

READ-ALOUDS

The Butterfly House
by Eve Bunting
(SCHOLASTIC)

Charlie the Caterpillar
by Dom Deluise
(SIMON & SCHUSTER)

From Caterpillar to Butterfly
by Deborah Heiligman
(HARPER TROPHY)

I Wish I Were a Butterfly
by James Howe
(GULLIVER BOOKS)

Monarch Butterfly
by Gail Gibbons
(HOLIDAY HOUSE)

PICTURE DICTIONARY WORDS

butterfly
caterpillar
leaves
skin
stem
chrysalis
cracks
flies
4 wings
scales
molting
color

POCKET CHART WORDS

Descriptive Story	**Sequence Story**
sky	lays eggs
crawl	hatch
eat leaves	tight
sunshine	sheds
warm	hardens
trees	metamorphosis

EMPHASIZE THESE HAVE-TO WORDS IN THIS THEME:

n+"u"   "Y"+l   K + 🏋+ d   👤+🏋+d   w + 🏋

new   **while**   **could**   **should**   **would**

(/k/ + muscle man +/d/)   (/sh/ + /oo/ + muscle man +/d/)   (/w/ + /oo/ + muscle man +/d/)

SENTENCE SQUARES SENTENCES

A caterpillar is fuzzy and hairy.
The caterpillar eats leaves and gets bigger.
A caterpillar loses its skin.
The caterpillar makes a chrysalis.
The butterfly has colorful scales.

SEQUENCE STORY PROMPT

Explain how a caterpillar turns into a butterfly.

Picture Dictionary Words

Directions: Read each word. Cut out the picture cards and glue them in your Picture Dictionary.

1. **butterfly**	2. **caterpillar**	3. **leaves**
4. sk+□ **skin**	5. **stem**	6. **chrysalis**
7. +s **cracks**	8. fl+ +s **flies**	9. **four wings**
10. **scales**	11. **molting**	12. **color**

Pocket Chart Words

Descriptive Story (Use with Let's Create It on page 124)

sk + 👁️	(crawling figure)	🟡 🍃🍃
sky	**crawl**	**eat leaves**
☀️ + 🤫 + 👁️ + n	w + (figure)	🌲🌲
sunshine	**warm**	**trees**

Sequence Story (Use with Sequence Story on page 128)

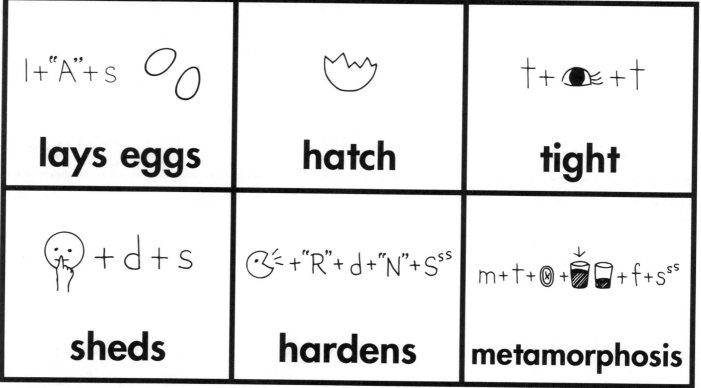

l + "A" + s ⬭⬭	(cracked egg)	† + 👁️ + †
lays eggs	**hatch**	**tight**
🤫 + d + s	+ "R" + d + "N" + s^ss	m + † + 🔘 + 🥛🥛 + f + s^ss
sheds	**hardens**	**metamorphosis**

Rebus Writing • Spring © 2004 Creative Teaching Press

Name _____

Word Hunt

Directions: Use your Picture Dictionary to help you find the word that goes with each picture. Write the correct word below each picture. Complete the special sentence at the bottom of the page.

    $Sk + \boxed{\bullet}$ ↙

- -

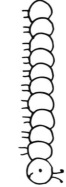  $fl + \bullet + S$

- -

  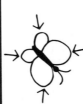 $+ S$

- -

   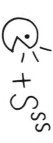 $+ S^{ss}$

- -

Rebus Writing • Spring © 2004 Creative Teaching Press

Secret Sentence Booklet

Directions: Write the correct word under each rebus picture.

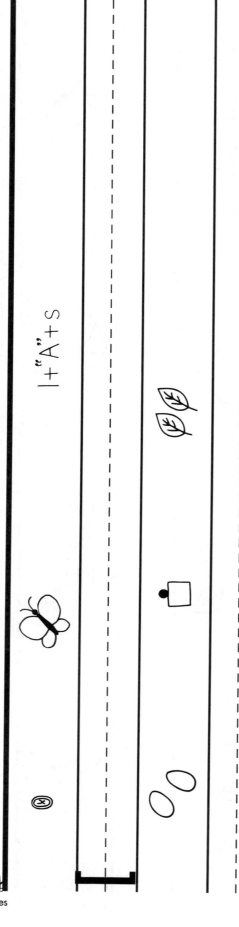

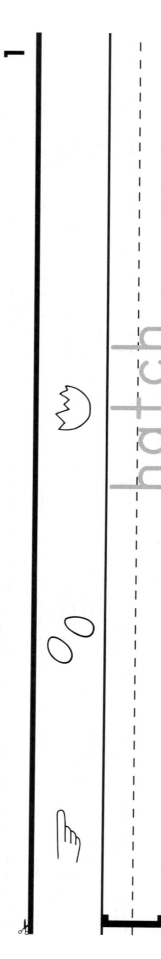

Rebus Writing • Spring © 2004 Creative Teaching Press

Secret Sentence Booklet

Directions: Write the correct word under each rebus picture.

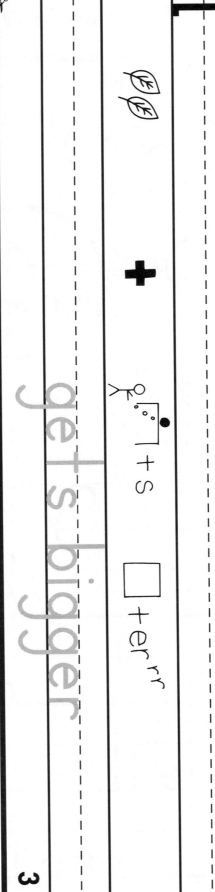

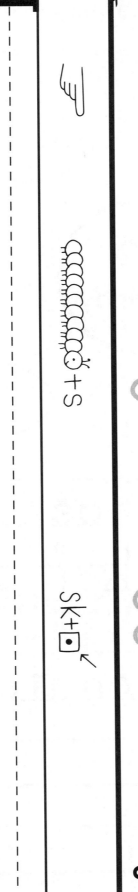

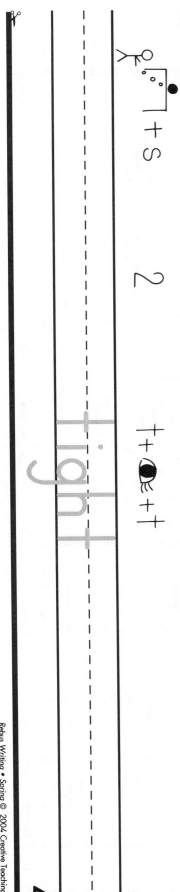

get s bigger

tight

3

4

Bubble Writing

Directions: Write the correct word next to each bubble. Use these words to complete the sentences at the bottom of the page.

Rebus Writing • Spring © 2004 Creative Teaching Press

Connect a Sentence

Directions: Read the phrase in the center bubble. Add words from the connecting bubbles to the phrase to make a sentence. Use additional words to create more sentences. Write the sentences on a separate piece of paper.

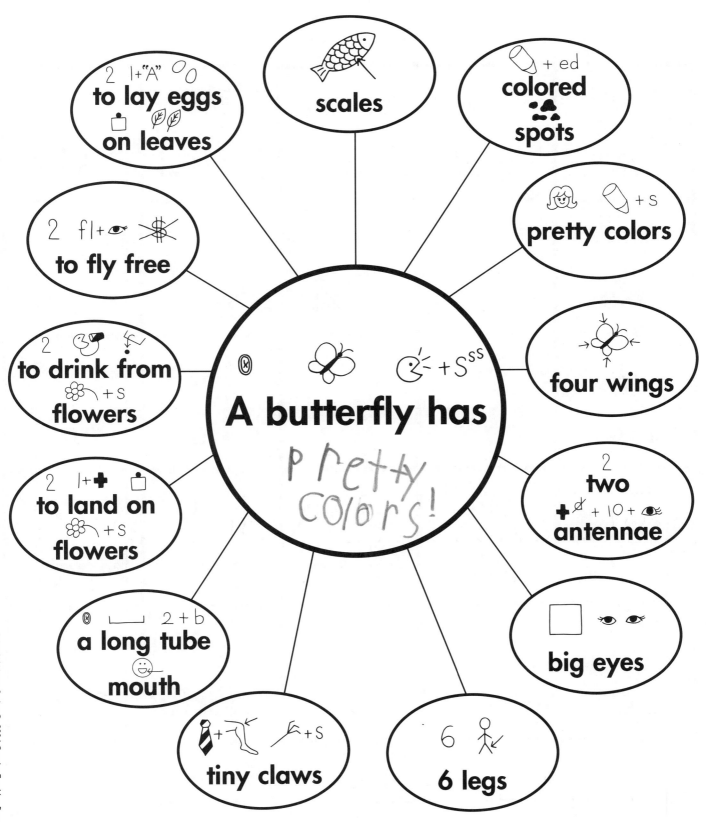

Sentence Squares

Directions: Read the word cards. Cut apart the cards and mix them up. Make sure that the words are face up. Use the word cards to make sentences.

A	caterpillar	leaves	skin
loses	is	butterfly	fuzzy
and	eats	The	its	has
hairy	scales	makes	gets	bigger
chrysalis	.	colorful	a

Rebus Writing • Spring © 2004 Creative Teaching Press

Sentence/Story Builder

Directions: Use the pictures to help you write a sentence or story that describes who, what, when, where, and why.

When	Who	Is Doing What	Where	Why
one day	caterpillar	changes	inside a chrysalis	butterfly

One day a silly caterpillar

named Nadine turned into

a silly butterfly.

Name _Alyssa_

Story Box

Directions: Use the picture box ideas to write a story.

Character	Setting
 butterfly	 leaves on a tree

1	2	3
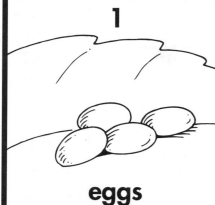 eggs	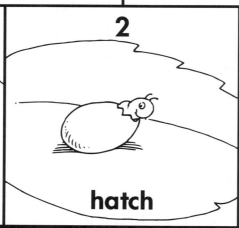 hatch	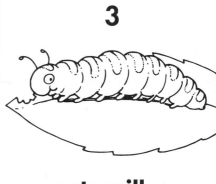 caterpillar

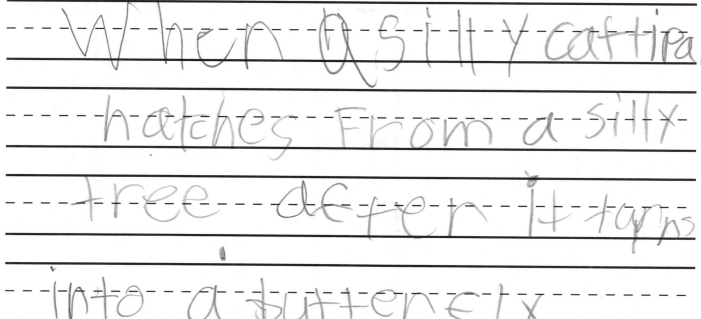

When a silly cattipalr
hatches From a silly
tree after it tarns
into a butterfly

Rebus Writing • Spring © 2004 Creative Teaching Press

Backward Story

Directions: Read the ending of the story and then tell what might have happened at the beginning and in the middle of the story.

QUESTIONS FOR PROMPTING
• What did the caterpillar look like?
• What did it lose? Why?
• What happened when its body hardened?
• What happened next?

_____

- -

_____

- -

_____

- -

_____

- -

_____

- -

_____

And   that's   how   a   caterpillar   became

a   butterfly.

Rebus Writing • Spring © 2004 Creative Teaching Press

Let's Create It

(Note to the teacher: Copy a class set of the Spring Finger Puppets on tagboard or white construction paper.)

MATERIALS

- ✓ tagboard or white construction paper
- ✓ crayons or markers
- ✓ scissors
- ✓ tape
- ✓ glue
- ✓ Picture Dictionary
- ✓ Descriptive Story Pocket Chart Words reproducible (page 114)

STEP 1

Color and cut out the bee, ladybug, butterfly, and caterpillar. Cut out the strips of paper, and roll each strip to create a "tube." Size each tube so that it fits around your pointing finger. Tape the end of each strip of paper. Glue each bug to a tube to create four finger puppets.

STEP 2

Use your Picture Dictionary and the pocket chart words to help you write a sentence or story about your bugs on a separate piece of paper.

Spring Finger Puppets

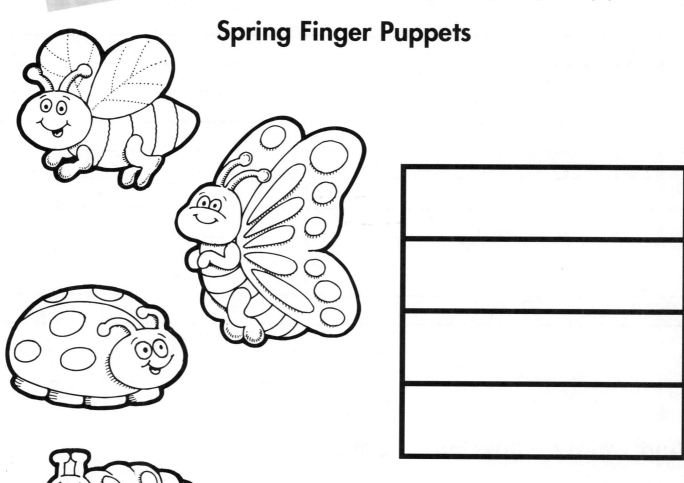

Shape Book

Directions: Color your cover. Cut out the cover and writing paper to create a shape book.

Word Web

Directions: Use the words on the word web to help you write a story.

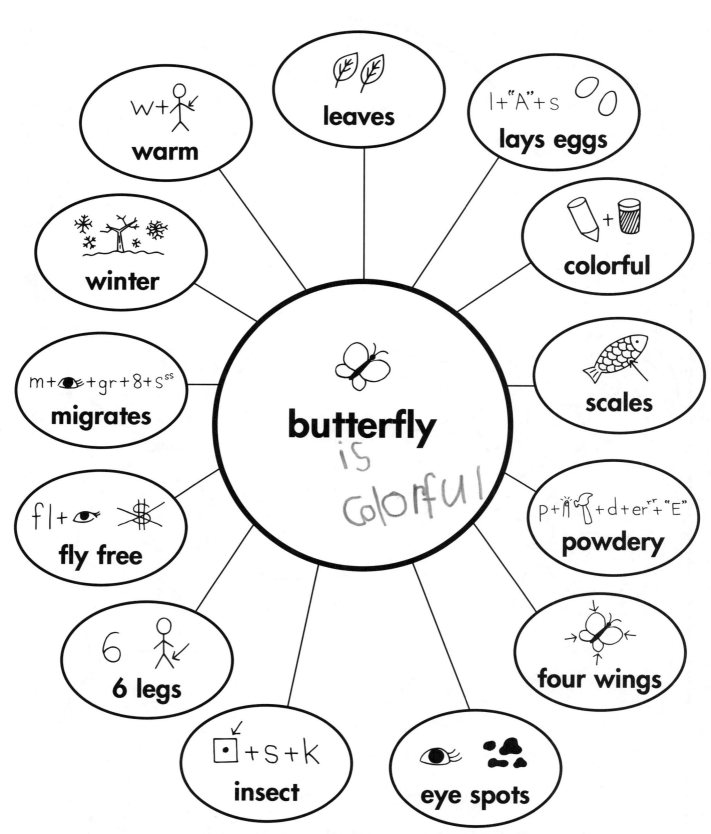

Rebus Writing • Spring © 2004 Creative Teaching Press

Class Book

Directions: Use words from your Picture Dictionary and around the room to help you complete the sentences. Draw a picture to go with your sentences.

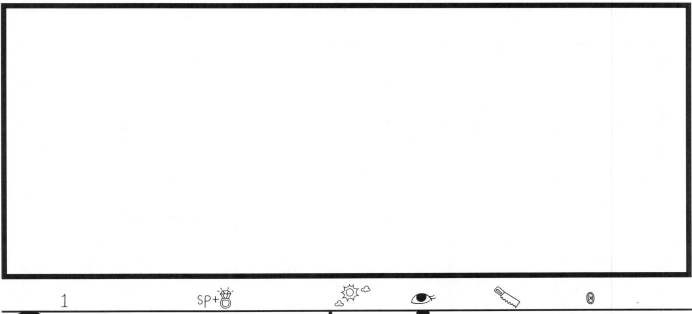

One spring day I saw a
butterfly crack open and
a ___mom___ flew out. It
looked ___sad___ and ___maa___.
It had ___spts___ and ___more sad___.
Then it ___cryd___.

By ___Milee___

Sequence Story

Directions: Color the pictures and cut them out. Glue the picture cards in order in the numbered boxes to show the life cycle of a butterfly. Use the picture cards to write a story on another piece of paper. Use your Picture Dictionary and the Sequence Story Pocket Chart Words to help you.

1	**2**	**3**
4	**5**	**6**